THE JOY OF DANCE

CAROLE EDRICH

summersdale

THE JOY OF DANCE

Summersdale Publishers Ltd
46 West Street
Chichester
West Sussex
PO19 1RP
UK

www.summersdale.com

Printed and bound in the Czech Republic

ISBN: 978-1-84953-637-0

Substantial discounts on bulk quantities of Summersdale books are available to corporations, professional associations and other organisations. For details contact Nicky Douglas by telephone: +44 (0) 1243 756902, fax: +44 (0) 1243 786300 or email: nicky@summersdale.com.

CONTENTS

INTRODUCTION

'Dance is the song of the body.'
Martha Graham

Dance gives us joy in so many ways. Spontaneous or choreographed, improvisational or rigidly formal, dance enables us to communicate in a way that needs no words. It can cross boundaries or create its own language; be a simple repetitive movement or a seemingly inchoate amalgam of styles. From the cutting edge of creativity to the essence of the reassuringly traditional, dance reflects extremes of intensity and emotion, and can be a fun, easy experience or as demanding of its proponents as an Olympic sport.

People have danced since before records began, which is why the true beginnings of dance are veiled in mystery. Some believe that the oldest dance-related remains at the Bhimbetka rock shelters of Madhya Pradesh, India, are around 9,000 years old, while depictions of Egyptian dancers in tombs painted around 3,300 years ago are considered to be the first real evidence of dance.

Dance forms evolved with the people who performed them; to continue traditions, commemorate events and commune with the gods, but also to be a part of something wonderful, social and fun to share. The movement of dance didn't have a unified beginning; instead different communities and cultures all over the world had their own distinct ideas about dance and the reason why there are so many different disciplines, styles and moves. Japanese Kyomai dance is intensely formal and elegant because it was influenced by the sophisticated manners of the Imperial Court at Kyoto in the seventeenth century, while Zimbabwe's Mbira dance is much looser and not formally organised because the Shona people, whose ancestors can be traced from the Iron Age, believe that their movements are influenced by the gods.

Not only was the beginning of dance diverse, but over the years it has continued to change and branch out. For example, heavy Renaissance dresses meant that court dances allowed more flexibility and movement above the waist, and more recently flamenco dancers adapted skirts with trails that were fashionable at the time into the *bata de cola*, which inspired a new type of elegant dancing.

While traditional dances are still performed in the pure form, others are a little more flexible. Proponents of one form of dance will have been taught in classes of another form, leading to new dance types arising all the time until they are innumerable.

Although for a while dance seemed to be an interest relegated to a privileged few, nowadays everyone loves it, and dance is seen as an integral part of our cultures as well as being beneficial to our health in numerous ways. With the formation of the UK's first All Party Parliamentary Dance Group in 2006, it became evident that politicians recognised the importance of dance, not just as art but in our culture, our society and for our health. Although dance is too wonderfully varied for these pages to include a detailed listing of each and every type there is, this book will lead you to discover dances from different countries and

cultures, and learn about their history, future and appearance in film and media. It will entertain you with unusual facts and quirky trivia, and reveal the stars who can dance like professionals.

Like all subject matter of such artistic, cultural and practical significance, dance is awash with interesting characters and anecdotes. I was once told the story of a young dancer caught skinny dipping in a lake near his famous ballet school, and another at the same school where, during a visit from Princess Margaret, security sniffer dogs led guards to a hidden stash of chocolate under one of the pupils' beds. The first of these was Wayne Sleep and the second Darcey Bussell. I wonder what became of them!

Starting with luck

Saying 'break a leg' to wish dancers luck is an old tradition, supposed to infer the opposite, just as saying 'good luck' is implied to mean 'bad luck'. Among some professional dancers the traditional saying isn't 'break a leg' but 'merde'.

FITNESS AND
HEALTH IN DANCE

*'Dance… like sport trains the body, increases its potential
for physical intelligence, accuracy, strength, speed,
alignment and develops kinaesthetic awareness.'*

SHOBANA JEYASINGH

Dance is fun. It's a liberating art form that can make your spirit soar, reveal hidden creativity, unite generations and cultures and inspire or rekindle romance. While there are specially created exercise dances such as Zumba (a combination of Latin and aerobic dance), Barre-core (aerobic and dance exercise using the classical ballet barre), Jazzercise (exercise with a jazz groove), Kelta Fit (a Scottish dance-based workout) and Bokwa (a combination of South African fighting dance), other purer types are just as effective for health and fitness. In fact, where studies have introduced dance to groups of people to see if they benefit medically, participants have enjoyed it so much that they have carried on with it, even when the trial is over. Today over 4.8 million people per year regularly attend community dance groups in the UK, but why are so many people choosing dance to keep fit instead of sticking to the traditional forms of exercise?

- Provides a great mind-body workout, keeping the body and the brain healthier and stimulating the production of chemicals that encourage nerve cell growth

- Improves heart and lungs, increasing aerobic fitness

The saddle or the stage?

A variety of surveys throughout the world have established that dancing is better than cycling for those recovering from, or being treated for various serious heart conditions.

- Encourages the development of stronger bones and reduces the risk of osteoporosis

- Increases coordination, agility and flexibility

Limbering up

A study at Washington University in Missouri, USA, showed that the Argentinian tango improved mobility of Parkinson's disease sufferers more than an exercise class.

- Improves balance and enhances spatial awareness

- Improves the metabolism by stimulating the production of high-density lipoproteins (HDL – good cholesterol) and reducing the production of low-density lipoproteins (LDL – bad cholesterol)

- Boosts confidence

- Remembering dance steps and sequences boosts brainpower by improving memory skills

- Improves cognitive activity

Therapy for the mind

Various studies in New York, US and Perth, Western Australia, established that while most physical activities don't help ward off dementia, ballroom dancing does, and that it increases cognitive acuity of all ages.

- Stimulates the production of serotonin, which reduces stress, regulates the appetite, encourages sleep, memory, learning and temperature regulation

- Perfect setting to meet new friends and being socially engaged leads to increased happiness and, in turn, a stronger immune system.

Dancers are fitter than top-level athletes!

An investigation published by the University of Hertfordshire in the UK discovered that members of the Royal Ballet were better than a group of international and national swimmers in seven out of ten health- and fitness-related areas.

Superstition: getting in the zone

Dance is a demanding discipline and some people use the same routine to get themselves 'in the zone' for their performance. This works in the same way as someone preparing to meditate going through the same routine to relax, or someone doing martial arts warming up to get themselves ready for a big competition. Some dancers might have very precise costume routines, such as doing hair or make-up in a certain sequence, others might want to touch a lucky charm or link fingers before their performance, or step on to the stage with their wrong foot so that when their cue comes they know to step in with the correct one. Some people might see this as a set of superstitions, but others see it as a form of neuro-linguistic programming (NLP) – a way of developing habits that make you more successful in your chosen endeavours.

CHAPTER 2

BALLET, BAREFOOT AND WITH FEELING

'Dance first. Think later. It's the natural order.'
SAMUEL BECKETT

As you would expect with any creative activity, some participants take joy in perfecting the classical forms, while others are driven to explore how they might take things further. This is true with ballet, which began with formal rules and traditional techniques but has also branched out into other dance forms, such as contemporary dance, modern dance and Tanztheater (a style of expressionist dance originating in Germany in the 1920s).

Classical ballet

'Ballet didn't become less mysterious to me. It became more so.'
MIKHAIL BARYSHNIKOV

What's it all about?

The beauty of classical ballet – the most formal of the ballet styles and one that adheres to traditional ballet technique – is in the interpretation of the movement language. Since this is sometimes extremely subtle (in that it is interpretation of the choreography rather than the choreography itself), in-depth knowledge of the dance is particularly rewarding. Classical ballet varies according to where it has been taught, the method used to teach it and the dancers themselves.

Despite there being a number of schools of ballet, each with its own philosophy, way of teaching and recognisable moves, there is a level of uniformity in the art. Thighs are rotated outwards from the hip, there are five basic leg positions from which every single movement is derived, and when performing jumps or leaps, classical ballet dancers strive to demonstrate *ballon,* the appearance of briefly floating in air.

Ballet: a brief history

1638 Birth of Louis XIV is celebrated with an elaborate dance performance.

1653 Louis XIV stars as Apollo in an elaborate 12-hour spectacle called *Le Ballet de la Nuit.*

1661 Louis XIV creates a dance school.

1670 Pierre Beauchamp creates the five ballet positions that are still used today.

1708 Russian dancers start performing ballets in public theatres.

1738 Russian Imperial Ballet is founded.

1739 Marie Sallé becomes the first female choreographer to perform in her own choreography, wearing a light, flowing robe and changing dance costume radically.

1740 Marie Camargo develops Marie Sallé's innovations, changing the costume to show the lines of her arch and ankles, wearing tights that cling to her leg shape and wearing the ballet slipper in favour of heels, which she is credited with inventing.

1748 Danish Royal Ballet is founded.

1760 Choreographer Jean-Georges Noverre writes about his efforts to expand ballet into a form of art called *ballet d'action* that uses physical expression and bodies to tell a story.

1780s Auguste Vestris lays the foundations for modern ballet technique in Paris. He teaches many dancers, including August Bournonville and Marius Petipa.

1820 The pointe shoe is created, from which came the *en pointe* position and the creation of the prima ballerina.

1822 Ballerina Marie Taglioni makes her debut in Vienna, becoming one of the first women to dance *en pointe*.

1831 Audiences are stunned by the blasphemous episode The Ballet of the Nuns (the first ballet blanc, where dancers wear traditional white, and the first romantic ballet) in the opera *Robert le Diable*.

1871 Marius Petipa becomes ballet master at the Imperial Ballet of St Petersburg; he retains this position for many years and trains a number of dancers.

1909 Expatriate Russian Serge Diaghilev forms the Ballets Russes in Paris, luring away Imperial Ballet of St Petersburg's chief choreographer Michel Fokine and star dancers from the company, among them Vaslav Nijinsky.

***c.*1910** Many dance critics start to question the trauma caused to ballerinas' bodies due to dancing *en pointe*. Companies begin to shift towards 'barefoot ballet', considered the beginning of contemporary dance.

1922 Ballet is used as a political tool in the Soviet Union. Works include 1927's *The Red Poppy*.

1929 Serge Lifar brings the Paris Opéra Ballet and ballet in France back to life after its decline in the late nineteenth century.

1934 George Balanchine forms the School of American Ballet, which will go on to become the New York City Ballet.

1956 Sadler's Wells is given its Royal Charter and becomes the Royal Ballet, from which two choreographers are to make their mark: Frederick Ashton and Kenneth MacMillan.

2014 Major companies the Royal Ballet and New York City Ballet continue to invest in new choreographers, such as Wayne McGregor and Christopher Wheeldon, while also preserving their heritage works.

Ballet is intoxicating and exhilarating to watch and takes extraordinary dedication to learn. Classical ballets can entrance you, transporting you to other worlds, full-length ballets tell fantastic stories, sometimes a short ballet makes you stop and think, while contemporary and modern ballets can intrigue you, evoking feelings or impressions through subtle use of sets of formal movements ('movement vocabulary') that haven't stopped developing since ballet's birth.

Aesthetics: stylistic variations include:

French
Russian Romantic
Contemporary British Classical
Italian Danish
Neoclassical

Each training method has a unique style, and many good teachers add elements of one method to the base of another, thereby creating something unique in terms of art, movement and atmosphere.

Preparing to dance: the ballet lesson

1. Every ballet class begins at the barre, a handrail at waist height that dancers use for support when they are warming up.

2. The *enchaînement*, the middle part of the class where the students learn steps and choreographies, is split into sections, such as the *adage*, the *petit allegro* and the *grand allegro*.

The discipline of the structured lesson helps the dancer to exercise all of their muscles, and develop a feel for their body while improving flexibility, grace and precision.

> ### Did you know?
>
> *White Lodge Museum & Ballet Resource Centre, in the centre of London's leafy Richmond Park, is the first dedicated ballet museum in the UK and home to the Royal Ballet Lower School. Prior to this Grade I-listed building becoming a ballet school, White Lodge was a royal residence, Edward VIII was born there, it is the address given on Queen Elizabeth II's birth certificate and it has been home to three serving prime ministers.*

The pointe shoe: where it began

In 1681, when women first danced ballet, they did so in heels and it wasn't until the mid-eighteenth century that Marie Camargo became the first ballerina to wear flat shoes. At first pointe shoes were simply ballet slippers that supported the foot with no more than ribbons. These helped the female dancer to briefly stand on her toes to appear weightless, sneakily assisted by a male partner dressed in black or even by a type of machine that held the person from behind, making them appear to float!

In 1822 Marie Taglioni was the first person to dance *en pointe*. The shoes she wore, which had the addition of heavy darning at the tip in order to support her weight, were a slight improvement on the flat shoes Marie Camargo had performed in. The next development came much later, in the late nineteenth century, with dancers like Pierina Legnani wearing shoes supported by padding and a much stronger sole.

The creation of modern pointe shoes has been attributed to Anna Pavlova who, in the twentieth century, stiffened and padded her shoe, while flattening the point to turn it into a kind of box, in order to make dancing more comfortable for her delicate arches.

Nowadays special reinforced pointe shoes are available, but dancing *en pointe* is difficult because the body's entire weight is borne by a very small area, even when the ballerina weighs less than 100 lb. While it is rare, men also occasionally dance *en pointe*, but since they tend to be considerably heavier than female ballet dancers, they must develop sufficient strength in the arch and ankles to do so, and for many it's either not worth the trouble or it is simply too difficult to build that type of strength in their feet. However, there have been some exceptions; in *A Midsummers Night's Dream*, Bottom is always danced by a man in pointe shoes and *Les Ballets Trockadero de Monte Carlo* (a set of playful parodies of dances by men who love the dances) is always *en pointe*. Contrary to popular opinion, some male dancers, including Mikhail Baryshnikov, have argued that teaching men to dance *en pointe* has many benefits, including improving strength and balance, and the ability to better relate to their female counterparts, having experienced how it feels.

Did you know?

Marie Camargo was the first woman to perform the entrechat-quatre *(jump, right thigh beats left, legs out, left thigh beats right).*

Modern and contemporary dance

*'It gives you nothing back... but that single
fleeting moment when you feel alive.'*

MERCE CUNNINGHAM

What's it all about?

Modern dance started out as a rebellion against classical ballet, favouring the expression of strong feelings as opposed to storytelling. Contemporary dance, in its myriad forms, comprises boundary-breaking performances by incorporating a continuously growing set of techniques influenced by modern dance that is often choreographed for very small groups of dancers. In contemporary and modern dance, tutus, pointe shoes (in some cases any shoes) are cast away in favour of a more creative wardrobe.

In the late nineteenth century Isadora Duncan broke away from the original constraints of ballet, getting rid of tutus and corsets in the process. Later, in the twentieth century, Martha Graham developed an angular, rooted style, while at the same time Merce Cunningham (working with composer and life partner John Cage) pushed the boundaries again. Cunningham's creations were often independent of sound, sets and costumes, and included formalised elements of chance, such as letting the roll of a dice determine what choreography, music and lighting should be used in a specific performance.

Their ideas soon spread to Europe where Rudolf von Laban invented dance analysis, a theory of movement and a system of notation. Later, in the 1960s, Robert Cohan founded the London Contemporary Dance School, training choreographers such as Richard Alston and Siobhan Davies.

In the 1960s and 1970s contemporary dance assimilated ideas from the worlds of film, music, visual arts and more, resulting in the huge, ever-evolving diversity of dances we see today. While certain countries and troupes have a reputation for particular styles, today's global environment has engendered such a fusion of disciplines and philosophies that we can no longer find borders.

What is Tanztheater?

While it is simple to define the principles of ballet, modern dance and Tanztheater allow more freedom in their choreographies. Like any other kind of dance, modern dance requires training, but there are no set positions to follow or specific steps to learn. Early purists had no intention of creating upright postures or airy impressions but worked a lot on the floor; now even that is evolving in as many different ways as there are choreographers to imagine them.

Aesthetics: some of the most significant styles are:

Graham
Cunningham
Limón
Release

Cunningham technique

Named after Merce Cunningham, this technique focuses on the architecture and interaction of the body and music in space and makes use of chance in developing choreographic phrases. Cunningham used the idea of the body's own 'line of energy' to promote easy, natural movement – something that English choreographer Richard Alston also employs.

Graham technique

Martha Graham described her dances as stylised forms of movement, often stopping in mid-air, using words like 'nervous', 'sharp' and 'zigzag', all of which were a representation of the times when she was choreographing. The style is very grounded, characterised by floor work, and the use of abdominal and pelvic contractions. Over time she softened the exercises to reduce the rigidity of the dance.

Limón technique

José Limón's technique focuses on the movement of breath through the body, the dynamic use of weight in each body part and the fluid succession of one movement into the next. The feeling of weight and 'heavy energy' in the body is achieved by executing swings through the body to create and suspend movement.

Release technique

Associated with therapeutic movement researches that make use of, or come from medical knowledge, these techniques enhance the level of self-awareness with which the dancer moves. Rather than just following physical exercises they create a set of practices that re-educates mind and body continuously.

Dress: Pointe shoes are never worn (feet are bare or in soft shoes that have good connection with the floor), there are no tutus or ballet shoes and anything goes in terms of clothing as dancers let their feelings become their costumes. One such dance was performed at Sadler's Wells in 2014 when French choreographer Olivier Dubois stripped the nine men and nine women of his company both literally and figuratively, to explore in hypnotic style where each of their bodies and souls met. The name of the choreography, which gave a clue as to what happens at the tribally thrilling ending, is *Tragédie*.

Did you know?

Groundbreaking choreographer Merce Cunningham started using the choreography software DanceForms in 1991.

Preparing to dance: cross-training

As the science of the body improves and dancers and teachers the world over continue to learn from each other, the way people prepare to dance becomes increasingly similar – although each warm-up will include movements close to those the dancer will perform.

These days almost all dancers cross-train as it keeps people stronger, healthier and more resilient. For example people involved in ballet or contemporary dance might start the morning with a ballet, yoga or Pilates class (some will start earlier in the gym), they'll have rehearsals throughout the day and if they don't have a show that night they'll go back to the gym or to Pilates or yoga. Training in classical ballet is used as a foundation or strength and technique developer for many other dance styles, too.

Tanztheater

> *'Each phase of a movement, every small transference*
> *of weight, every single gesture of any part of the*
> *body reveals some feature of our inner life.'*
> RUDOLF VON LABAN

What's it all about?

Tanztheater is a development of modern and contemporary dance. It rarely has a conventional narrative plot; instead trained dancers use dance and theatrical methods to stimulate the audience to a certain train of thought. Rudolf von Laban coined the word – already in use by members of the German expressionist movement in the 1910s and 1920s – to describe the dance form he was to create.

Aesthetics: an amalgam of styles that the choreographer and dancer pick to investigate:

ideas thoughts
feelings emotions
impressions
meanings experiences

That is why the famous Trinity Laban Conservatoire in London's Greenwich teaches music as well as dance, and techniques as different as jazz dance, hip hop and flamenco.

Dress: Anything goes, including props and even nakedness!

Did you know?

On the day that famous Tanztheater choreographer Pina Bausch died (aged 68, five days after being diagnosed with lung cancer) her company decided to perform in Poland despite the news. Fernando Suels Mendoza, who had been with the company for 17 years, felt it was the only option. In Bausch's own words, 'Dance, dance, otherwise we are lost'.

Ballet and modern dance game changers

'"Keep the feet in!" shouted Rudolf Nureyev who knew I had misframed a shot even though he was dancing. We were shooting Giselle *at ATV Elstree. Didn't ever make that mistake again!'*

JEREMY HOARE

Who were the most influential ballet and modern dance personalities? Should they be chosen for their fame, actions, influence, poise, power or the poignancy of their creations? Take a look at this selection of people connected to ballet, modern and contemporary dance, and you'll see that it's a combination of skills, actions, hard work, deep thought and commitment that make these people truly great.

Dancers

Isadora Duncan
1877–1927

Angela Isadora Duncan is considered an icon of freedom, since she refused to be constrained by academic dance or social convention, instead taking inspiration from the classics, architecture, language and philosophy. She took ballet lessons at home during her Californian childhood before moving to Chicago and then London, Paris and Russia. She toured with Loie Fuller, pioneer of theatrical lighting and contemporary dance, and initiated what developed into modern dance, particularly the idea that dance comes from within, while doing away with tutus and corsets. She died aged 50, when her scarf got caught up in the wheels of the car she was travelling in, breaking her neck.

Best known for: Breaking conventions of classical ballet and society, and adopting some of the basic tenets of modern dance.

Anna Pavlova
1881–1931

This Russian prima ballerina performed at the Mariinsky Ballet and briefly with Sergei Diaghilev's Ballets Russes. She enjoyed the touring life, especially when she formed her own company, which toured in countries that had never before seen ballet.

Best known for: Her signature role in Michel Fokine's classical ballet *The Dying Swan* and introducing ballet to so many new places.

Darcey Bussell
Born: 1969

Darcey Bussell started her professional dancing career at Sadler's Wells but after just one year, at the age of 20, moved to the Royal Ballet to become their youngest ever principal dancer. She remained loyal to the Royal Ballet for the rest of her career, but performed as a guest with prestigious companies to audiences all over the world. Although she retired in 2007 she is still very committed to the dance world, and is president or patron of a large number of important English, Australian, New Zealand and international dance organisations, including the Royal Academy of Dance. She joined the BBC's *Strictly Come Dancing* panel in 2012 and co-presented the BBC's *Young Dancer 2015*.

Best known for: Her dedication to dance, in appreciation of which she has been given several prestigious awards.

Best of the rest

Classical ballet:
Vaslav Nijinsky
Rudolf Nureyev
Margot Fonteyn
Carlos Acosta
Natalia Makarova.

Chorographers and innovators

Rudolf von Laban
1879–1958

Born in Hungary, Rudolf von Laban was a pioneer of modern dance, and explored the theory and practice of dance and of movement in general. He set up schools in Germany and England, and invented a system of dance notation that is still used today. True to his spirit – Laban believed that his dancers should have a very diverse background – the Trinity Laban Conservatoire of Music and Dance was formed by the consolidation of Trinity College of Music and the Laban Dance Centre in 2005.

Best known for: His Laban technique, notation and his Tanztheater works.

Martha Graham
1894–1991

Born in Pittsburgh, USA, Martha Graham was influenced by her father, a doctor who believed that a body could express its inner senses. She took up dancing aged 22 – widely considered to be very late – when she joined the Denishawn School of Dancing and Related Arts founded by Ruth St Denis and her husband Ted Shawn. Her company has included famous dancers such as Alvin Ailey, Twyla Tharp, Paul Taylor and Merce Cunningham, and her work has been performed by Margot Fonteyn, Rudolf Nureyev, Mikhail Baryshnikov and Liza Minnelli, among others.

Best known for: Being the mother of modern dance and creating a theory and language of movement still used today.

George Balanchine
1904–1983

George Balanchine, who became choreographer for Sergei Diaghilev's Ballets Russes when he was 21, created ten ballets including *Apollo* and *The Prodigal Son*. A few years after Diaghilev died, he was invited to the USA by Lincoln Kirstein to create the School of American Ballet in New York City. Balanchine was a radical choreographer for his time and is famous for his plotless ballets, which were considered too daring by some at the time. After going solo he started creating dances for Broadway musicals and Hollywood films and formed the Ballet Society, which was later named the New York City Ballet.

Best known for: Plotless ballets and starting the New York City Ballet and the School of American Ballet.

Pina Bausch
1940–2009

It is said that German-born Philippina 'Pina' Bausch learnt to observe people and their motivations while working at her parents' hotel in Solingen, Germany. She danced at the Solingen Children's Ballet as a child, moving to the Folkwang School in Essen. The schoolmaster Kurt Jooss taught Pina and the other students modern dance and the rules of classical ballet, with influences from opera, music, drama, sculpture, painting, photography and design, all of which can be seen in her later work. She founded Tanztheatre Wuppertal in 1973 and her works were often very dramatic, including talking, sound and the use of strange stage design and props.

Best known for: Her Tanztheatre work and being known as one of modern ballet's greatest innovators.

Did you know?

By introducing the ideas behind ballet d'action (which involves the expression of character and emotion through the dancers rather than costumes and props) Vincenzo Galeotti prepared the scene for the advent of romantic ballet.

Wayne Sleep
Born 1948

When Wayne Philip Colin Sleep was 13 he won a scholarship to the Royal Ballet School. He joined the Royal Ballet Company five years later and soon became a senior principal dancer, having numerous roles created for him by some of the best choreographers of our times. His own company, DASH, which he formed in 1980, was revolutionary for its day because it taught ballet, jazz, tap and contemporary dance, opening up dance to a much wider audience.

Best known for: Appearing on TV many times as a dancer, celebrity and actor, including *I'm a Celebrity Get Me Out of Here*, *Celebrity Come Dine With Me*, *Big Dance* and as a judge on the dance show *Stepping Out*.

Best of the rest

Classical ballet:	**Modern and contemporary dance:**
Mikhail Baryshnikov	Robert Cohan
Sir Frederick Ashton	Siobhan Davies
Michel Fokine	Trisha Brown
Sir Kenneth MacMillan	Twyla Tharp
John Neumeier.	Lester Horton
	José Limón
	Paul Taylor
	Bill T. Jones
	Ruth St Denis
	Richard Alston.

Principals, producers and directors

Sergei (Serge) Diaghilev
1872–1929

Although neither a choreographer nor a dancer, Sergei Diaghilev's company the Ballets Russes had a huge impact on ballet. The company broke new ground, used startlingly different movements and incorporated design and drama into their work in ways that, although then radical and new, have now become normal fare. Sometimes he even put more than one ballet on in an evening. These innovations made ballet more accessible and much more popular across Europe and the USA.

Best known for: His innovations in ballet.

Alicia Alonso
Born: 1921

Born in Cuba, Alicia Alonso learned flamenco as a child, then danced with the American Ballet Theatre before returning to Cuba in 1950. She established a company that went on to become the National Ballet of Cuba in 1955. When she was just 19 she became partially blind but overcame this by making sure her partners were exactly where she expected them to be and by using stage lights to guide herself.

Best known for: Creating the National Ballet of Cuba and her classical ballet performances of *Giselle* and *Carmen*.

Best of the rest

Classical ballet:
Dame Ninette de Valois
Joe Layton.

Modern and contemporary dance:
Mark Morris
Alvin Ailey.

The homes of ballet

'I believe that we learn by practice… Practice is a means of inviting the perfection desired.'

MARTHA GRAHAM

Most large companies found their own feeder schools, hand-picking the students from huge national or international outreach programmes, and it's often not sensible to consider the school without the company that it has been designed to feed. The desperately hard work involved in learning dance in addition to obligatory school lessons brings its own rewards; a wonderful *esprit* between pupils, a love and deep knowledge of their art and the feeling of having achieved a major step towards employment in the art one adores. However, of the talented few selected, even fewer make it to the companies themselves. The world's biggest ballet school, the Cuban National School of Ballet in Havana, was founded in 1931 and today has around 3,000 pupils; and there are a host of other prestigious academies, each of which has played its part in the development of the dancers of our times.

The Royal Ballet School, London

This famous school, which has produced generations of stars, was founded in 1926 as the Academy of Choreographic Art by Dame Ninette de Valois, who collaborated with Lilian Baylis, manager of the Old Vic theatre. In 1939 it merged with the Sadler's Wells company and school, named the Sadler's Wells Ballet and Sadler's Wells Ballet School, respectively. In 1946 the Sadler's Wells Ballet company moved to its first permanent home: the Royal Opera House in Covent Garden, while the Sadler's Wells Ballet School moved to Barons Court in 1947 where it established educational learning in addition to its vocational ballet training.

In 1956 a Royal Charter was granted and the companies were renamed the Royal Ballet School, the Royal Ballet and the Sadler's Wells Royal Ballet (when it moved to Birmingham in 1990 it was renamed Birmingham Royal Ballet). Then in 2003 the Barons Court campus moved to Covent Garden. Studios are now linked to the Royal Ballet by an architectural prize winner, the Bridge of Aspiration, which finally fulfilled Dame Ninette's dream: to have company and school side by side in central London.

Alumni include: Margot Fonteyn, Anya Linden, Kenneth MacMillan, Lynn Seymour, David Wall, Antoinette Sibley, Anthony Dowell, Marguerite Porter, Stephen Jefferies, Darcey Bussell, Jonathan Cope.

www.royalballetschool.org.uk

The Vaganova Academy of Russian Ballet, St Petersburg

One of the most famous and influential classical ballet schools in the world, and established in 1738, the Vaganova Academy of Russian Ballet has also been known as the Imperial Ballet School and the Leningrad State Choreographic Institute. It is named after Agrippina Vaganova, whose method of classic ballet training has been taught at the school since the 1920s. It is the associate school of the world-leading Mariinsky Ballet and many of the world's most prestigious ballet schools have adopted elements of the Vaganova method into their own training.

Alumni include: George Balanchine, Mikhail Baryshnikov, Michel Fokine, Vaslav Nijinsky, Rudolf Nureyev, Anna Pavlova.

www.vaganovaacademy.com

The School of American Ballet, New York

Established in 1934 by George Balanchine and philanthropist Lincoln Kirstein, who wrote that it had been founded for one purpose, 'To provide dancers as well trained as any other technician, whether it be surgeon, architect, or musician.' Famous Russians fleeing the Russian Revolution taught there, all sharing the intention to establish a major classical ballet company in America. It led to the formation of today's New York City Ballet and was awarded the National Medal of Arts by Barack Obama in 2009.

Alumni include: Sean Young, Ashlee Simpson, Macaulay Culkin, Vanessa Carlton, Kyra Nichols, Alan Bergman, Paloma Herrera, Wendy Whelan, Patrick Bissell, Patricia McBride, Tanaquil LeClercq, Heather Watts.

www.sab.org

The Bolshoi Ballet Academy, Moscow

One of the oldest and most prestigious ballet schools in the world, the Bolshoi Ballet Academy (also known as the Moscow State Academy of Choreography) is the affiliate school of the Bolshoi Ballet. It was founded as an orphanage by Catherine II in 1763, with the first dance classes given nine years later, and is Moscow's oldest theatrical school.

Alumni: Raisa Struchkova, Ekaterina Maximova, Nikolai Fadeyechev, Vladimir Vasiliev, Mikhail Lavrovsky.

www.bolshoiballetacademy.com

The Paris Opera Ballet School

The Paris Opera Ballet School celebrated its 300th birthday in 2013 and is the birthplace of classical academic ballet, having been founded by Louis XIV who created the Académie Royale de Danse in 1661. For a long time the school was based in the Opéra buildings, with living conditions so bad that the students were given the nickname *les petits rats de l'Opéra* ('little rats of the Opera'). This changed in 1987 when modern buildings in Nanterre united dance training, academic training and the boarding school.

Alumni: Pascal Molat, Dana Genshaft, Mathilde Froustey, Vincent Chaillet, Marcelo Gomes, Isabelle Ciaravola, Paulo Arrais, Laurent Guilbaud, Karl Paquette, David Hallberg.

www.operadeparis.fr

San Francisco Ballet School

San Francisco Ballet and the San Francisco Ballet School were both established in 1933 as a single institution by Gaetano Merola, founding director of the San Francisco Opera. The creation of this school – which taught ballet, tap, modern and interpretive dance – meant that San Francisco became the second city in the country, after New York, to have a ballet school attached to an established opera company. Although all-dance programmes (teaching a variety of dance) were occasionally presented before Willam Christensen became company ballet master, he was the person who made the school so well known for its dance.

Alumni: Tricia Albertson, Seth Orza, Kristin Long, Anita Paciotti, Yumiko Takeshima, Logan Learned, Ashley Ellis.

www.sfballet.org/balletschool

Canada's National Ballet School, Toronto

Founded by Celia Franca (who had been recommended by Dame Ninette de Valois) and Betty Oliphant, the National Ballet School (NBS) opened in 1951 with a building financed by Canada's National Ballet Guild. Modern dance was introduced in 1971 and the school celebrated its 25th anniversary while *Flamenco at 5.15*, a Canadian National Film Board documentary on flamenco classes at NBS, won an Academy Award for Best Documentary Film. The school moved to custom-built premises in 2005 which have since won 14 architectural awards.

Alumni: Jeroen Verbruggen, Evan Mckie, Brent Parolin, Crystal Costa, Yuriko Kajiya.

www.nbs-enb.ca

Did you know?

The three oldest ballet schools in the world are the Paris Opera Ballet School, the Vaganova Academy of Russian Ballet and the Royal Danish Ballet.

English National Ballet, London

Originally named the London Festival Ballet for the Festival of Britain, the English National Ballet was formed by Alicia Markova, Anton Dolin and Julian Braunsweg in 1950. The company toured England from the very start and toured internationally from 1951. This was financed by donations from private individuals and businesses until a new production of *Swan Lake* overran by such a long way that the company headed for bankruptcy. In the recovery that followed, theatre owner Donald Albery persuaded the Arts Council to subsidise the ballet and school in recognition of its work in bringing ballet to all corners of the UK. The school, which teaches classical ballet, and is run independently from the company, was founded in 1988.

Alumni: Erina Takahashi, George Williamson, Guilherme Duarte de Menezes, Ken Saruhashi

www.enbschool.org.uk

The Royal Danish Ballet School, Copenhagen

Within a year of the founding of the Royal Danish Ballet in 1771, the associated school was formed. One of its most influential masters was the Danish dancer August Bournonville who led the company between 1828 and 1879 and choreographed around 50 ballets, more than ten of which are still part of the company's repertoire. Highly influenced by French dance, Bournonville introduced high-quality Danish male dancers, raising the ballet to international acclaim while also giving it a unique style that remains to this day. After Bournonville's death in 1879, ballet master Hans Beck taught what he had learnt from his predecessor – this became known as the Bournonville style. Later, in expanding the company's repertoire, Harald Lander encouraged local choreographers to develop their skills, one of whom was Børge Ralov who choreographed the first modern Danish ballet, *The Window in the Mirror* in 1934, and trained many prominent international dancers.

Alumni: Erik Bruhn, Ulrik Birkkjaer, Eva Kloborg, Johan Kobborg. www.kglballetskole.dk

The Joffrey Ballet School, Chicago

In 1952 Robert Joffrey founded the Joffrey Ballet with Gerald Arpino in Chicago. Their combination of artistic direction and strong leadership pushed the company and school into its place as a vanguard of American dance education and classical ballet training. It's known for its hugely varied repertoire, which included choreographies as diverse as *Billboards* (a ballet featuring the works of Prince) to Michel Fokine's *Petrushka*, which was created more than a century ago. In 1956, when most companies were performing classical ballet, Arpino toured their six-dancer ensemble around the US in a big car and trailer, while Joffrey stayed behind and taught classes to earn the money for their wages. Invited by Jacqueline Kennedy, the Joffrey Company was the first to perform at the White House and Joffrey was presented with the prestigious Capezio Dance Award, and commended for his work with youth and the school.

Alumni: Harriet McMeekin, Rachel Rutherford, Laura DiOrio.
www.joffreyballetschool.com

The whims of romantic ballet

Vincenzo Galeotti, master of the Royal Danish Ballet School between 1775 and 1816, is believed to have choreographed the oldest ballet still performed – Amors og Balletmesterens Luner (Amor and the Ballet Master Luner).

Competitions

The world of ballet and classical dance is incredibly competitive, with large numbers of skilled artists competing for a few very sought-after jobs. Winning a top-level ballet competition can be pivotal in getting a young dancer recognised, or in affording someone a career-changing position. Some of the most important are:

- The Genée International Ballet Competition, named after The Royal Academy of Dance (RAD)'s first president Dame Adeline Genée which was first held in 1931

- The International Dance Association (IDA)'s Prix Benois which is held in Moscow and has UNESCO patronage and was started in 1991

- The Prix de Lausanne which began in 1973

- America's International Ballet Competition (USA IBC), the first of which took place in 1979.

Influential dances

Today's ballet, modern and contemporary dance scene is wonderfully varied, where new contemporary choreographies, reconstructions and some of the traditional favourites coexist. As choreographers experiment with old and new styles, more and more different dance forms are being brought into the mix. By placing the development of the dances themselves in date order, this section shows how our vibrant dance scene has developed.

1913 Diaghilev commissions Igor Stravinsky to compose a ballet about ancient rituals. From this came the short ballet, *The Rite of Spring*. Many other choreographers have created their own versions of this, including Shen Wei, whose dancers move to the music with no plot at all.

1928 George Balanchine's *Apollo* is considered to be the first neoclassical ballet.

1931 Martha Graham's work *Primitive Mysteries* deals with religion and ritual at a time when nobody else creates dances on serious themes.

1935 The first version of Prokofiev's ballet *Romeo and Juliet*, choreographed by Leonid Lavrovsky, is composed, and later premieres in 1940 at the Kirov (Mariinsky) Theatre. Many other dancers and choreographers have created versions – for example, in Kenneth MacMillan's choreography, which received 43 curtain calls and almost 40 minutes of applause when it was performed at Covent Garden in 1965.

1958 Agnes de Mille, who choreographed stories of American life in ballet and musical form (such as *Oklahoma!*), uses Morton Gould's original score for the short ballet *Fall River Legend* to portray a nineteenth-century scandal where spinster Lizzie Borden was accused of killing her parents.

1964 Frederick Ashton's one-act ballet *The Dream*, based on *A Midsummer Night's Dream* by William Shakespeare, with music by Felix Mendelssohn, premieres.

1967 George Balanchine's short plotless ballet *Jewels* is split into *Emeralds*, *Rubies* and *Diamonds*, each of which features a different composer.

1973 Twyla Tharp choreographs *Deuce Coupe*, a ballet to music by the Beach Boys, for the Joffrey Ballet. Using this sort of music for serious dance is a controversial and daring idea.

1976 Tharp's choreography for *Push Comes to Shove* is considered innovative for the combination of modern movements with pointe shoes and classically trained dancers.

1995 Matthew Bourne's *Swan Lake* makes headlines because all of the dancers are male.

2000 Modern dance choreographer Shen Wei's piece *Folding* is site specific (meaning the place is an important part of the performance). In it dancers slowly bend their bodies to the sound of Buddist chanting and John Tavener's music.

2000 Unlike most modern dance, Matthew Bourne's *Car Man* tells a story. However this story is a dark thriller, where the dancers perform barefoot or with work boots and the characters are clearly portrayed through the dance.

2014 Gandini Juggling's brand of juggling, ballet and modern dance produces a variety of exciting and groundbreaking works including *4 x 4 Ephemeral Architects*, a sparkling mix of juggling and classical ballet. In it, four classical ballet dancers, choreographed by former Royal Ballet first artist Ludovic Ondiviela, join four of Gandini's elite jugglers to create a crystalline architecture of fleeting journeys and object trails.

Small and silver screens

> *'To dance is to be out of yourself. Larger,*
> *more beautiful, more powerful.'*
> AGNES DE MILLE

Cinema, television and now the Internet have brought the world of dance into our lives. They allow us to glimpse the beauty of the perfectly trained bodies, pain, hard work and skills that produced it, and to experience the joy of the dance from the comfort of our own homes.

Save the Last Dance (2001)
Director: Thomas Carter

Sara (Julia Stiles) joins the Juilliard dance school to fulfil her dead mother's dream and becomes friends with her flat mates who introduce her to hip hop . Miles (Sean Patrick) ignites in her a passion for hip hop when they compose some music together. Although she idolises her ballet teacher she feels torn between the strict ballet technique and creative flexibility offered by hip hop, and some hard choices follow.

Fascinating fact: During the movie's opening credits, Sara is shown auditioning for Juilliard, which is misspelled as 'Julliard' on a sign outside the room where the audition is occurring.

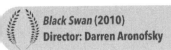

Black Swan (2010)
Director: Darren Aronofsky

Dancer Nina (Natalie Portman) competes for the part of the white swan in *Swan Lake* and is so overwhelmed by the pressure that she assumes more of the characteristics of the black swan.

Fascinating fact: While Portman studied ballet as a child and is said to have taken between 12 and 18 months to train for the part, American Ballet Theatre dancer Sarah Lane was her dance double (modern technology enabling Portman's face to be superimposed onto Lane's body). Several controversies arose. Some people refused to believe that Portman hadn't done all of the dancing (or that even 18 months of intensive training cannot create a ballerina), others were shocked at the extent to which modern technology was used and more were horrified that Lane wasn't in the film credits or thanked by Portman at the Oscars.

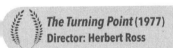

The Turning Point (1977)
Director: Herbert Ross

When her daughter joins a ballet company in New York City, former dancer Deedee is forced to confront her long-ago decision to give up the stage to have a family while friend Emma stayed on to become a prima ballerina. This is a fictionalised version of the friendship between ballerinas Isabel Mirrow Brown and Nora Kaye.

Fascinating fact: While many dance films of the time used actors, this film includes ballet dancer Mikhail Baryshnikov.

The Red Shoes (1948)
Directors: Michael Powell and Emeric Pressburger

A British feature film that is a story within a story. A young ballerina becomes the lead dancer in a new ballet called *The Red Shoes*, based on the Hans Christian Andersen fairytale of the same name. It features real-life dancers Robert Helpmann, Léonide Massine, Ludmilla Tchérina , Marius Goring, Moira Shearer and Anton Walbrook and is one of Martin Scorsese's all-time favourite films.

Fascinating fact: It is said to have been inspired by the meeting of Sergei Diaghilev and British ballerina Diana Gould. Diaghilev asked her to join his company but died before she was able to.

Pina (2011)
Director: Wim Wenders

A German documentary about the inspiring choreographer Pina Bausch, who died unexpectedly while the film was being prepared, causing Wenders to cancel its production – although he was persuaded by the cast to return to it at a later date. It showcases dancers of Bausch's company, Tanztheater Wuppertal, who talk about Bausch's influence around Wuppertal.

Fascinating fact: This feature-length dance documentary was considered revolutionary as it was filmed and released in 3D.

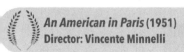

An American in Paris (1951)
Director: Vincente Minnelli

This romantic comedy, starring Gene Kelly (who was also the choreographer), Leslie Caron, Oscar Levant, Georges Guétary and Nina Foch, with a dream ballet sequence lasting an unprecedented 17 minutes, was the most expensive production number ever at the time, costing over $500,000.

Fascinating fact: The film was inspired by George Gershwin's 1928 orchestral composition of the same name.

Billy Elliot (2000)
Director: Stephen Daldry

Eleven-year-old Billy, played by Jamie Bell, is an aspiring dancer having to deal with negative stereotypes about male ballet dancers in north-east England during the 1984–85 miners' strike.

Fascinating fact: Jamie Bell was the only actor in the film local to the area in which it was set.

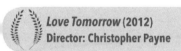

Love Tomorrow (2012)
Director: Christopher Payne

Set in London, ex-ballet dancer Eva (Cindy Jourdain) receives devastating news about her fiancé Dominic (Max Brown). She meets charismatic Cuban dancer Oriel (Arionel Vargas) and the two help each other face the most important dilemmas of their lives.

Fascinating fact: Produced by Emmy Award-winning film-makers and choreographers Balletboyz (Billy Trevitt and Michael Nunn).

CHAPTER 3

BALLROOM DANCE

> *'Ballroom is two people dancing together to music, touching in perfect harmony.'*
> ANTON DU BEKE

Ballroom dance is a sociable, fun and relaxed way to express oneself through dance, especially for novices, because the moves can be learnt in advance. From the subtle, gentle waltz to the flirtatious cha-cha, ballroom and Latin dance caters for all of your moods and there are plenty of places to learn.

What's it all about?

In its widest meaning, ballroom dancing, which has grown in popularity since the 1930s and has had a huge recent boost due to television dance competitions, is almost any type of partner dancing performed at social events. However, the advent of formal competitions and organisations to support and administer them has led to a more limited set of dances being considered. Sequence and formation dancing – where couples dance as part of larger groups, simultaneously performing the same moves in sequence and in different directions when dancing in formation – is still popular and other historical or national dances are danced in ballrooms or salons.

There are more than a hundred registered dance teacher organisations in England alone, each with its own dance technique rules and styles. They are important because each is allied to different governing bodies where dance is promoted in its own way, and the criteria for amateur and professional competitions reflect the rules and styles they support. In competitions judges mark the dancers on different aspects of their performance, including posture, timing, the way they move together, how their bodies are positioned as a couple and how well they cover the dance floor.

Aesthetics: In the UK ballroom dance can be grouped into two categories: modern ballroom style with dance types, such as the waltz and foxtrot, and Latin style, with dances adapted from original Latin grooves. In the US two additional styles are popular: American smooth and American rhythm, which combine elements of both. 'American' styles are only danced in America, while 'international' styles are actually European and only used by Americans to talk about non-American styles (Europeans just say 'ballroom' and 'Latin').

Dress: Ballroom dresses with full skirts for women and tailcoats with bow ties and shirts are most common in competition; social dancing has a more relaxed dress code and props are only used in shows (never in a social or competitive environment).

Ballroom dance: a brief history

Fifth-fifteenth centuries People in courtly life perform formal social dances like the carola (recorded in medieval literature and art).

Fourteenth-seventeenth centuries Tight-fitting clothing means that most Renaissance dancing uses complicated footwork but little upper-body movement.

1600-1750 Popular social dances are developed at the French Court, including the minuet and gavotte.

Early nineteenth century Women start wearing softer dresses, which allows greater freedom of movement and begins the creation of lively dances like the polka.

1816 The British Prince Regent (later George IV) first allows waltzes at his society balls.

1830s Johann Strauss II becomes known as the Waltz King due to the huge numbers of waltz tunes he composes and performs.

1909 First World Ballroom Dance Championships are held by Camille de Rhynal in Paris.

1920s-1930s Jazz and other new music forms lead to new types of dancing.

1930s-1940s Standard rules are introduced for competitive dances.

1992 *Strictly Ballroom* hits film screens.

2004 *Strictly Come Dancing* debuts on UK television, followed by a host of other programmes celebrating competitive and social dance in its myriad forms, changing the way ballroom and Latin dancing is seen by millions.

> **Did you know?**
>
> In the famous fairy tale, Cinderella's first dance was a waltz.

Smooth standard

The couple move around the dance floor in an anticlockwise direction, smoothly transitioning between patterns. Examples are:

Foxtrot
Quickstep Waltz
Viennese waltz

Latin

These energetic dances to a syncopated rhythm are based closely on the original Latin and Spanish dance formats. The swing, rumba, cha-cha, salsa and mambo are danced on the spot, samba and the paso doble progress anticlockwise across the dance floor. Find out more in Chapter 6 and in the table on pages 58–60.

Rumba

Considered the sexiest of the five Latin American ballroom dances, the rumba tells a story of love, passion and excitement between the dancers through swaying motions, sharp eye contact and intimate body language. Ballroom rumba is not to be confused with Afro-Cuban rumbas

– which often take the shorthand form 'rumba' – as they are very different types of dance (although Ballroom rumba has very much been influenced by Cuban life and culture). Some movements from both have names that reflect the fact they depict daily tasks of the Cuban people, such as 'shoeing the mare', 'doing the laundry/dishes', 'climbing a rope' or 'the courtship of barnyard fowls'.

Waltz

*'Endearing Waltz! - to thy more melting tune…
Waltz - Waltz alone - both legs and arms demands,
Liberal of feet, and lavish of her hands.'*

LORD BYRON, FROM 'THE WALTZ'

What's it all about?

The waltz is a smooth dance, usually in phrases of three, to a 3/4 time and 90 beats to the minute, performed by a couple as they revolve around each other and anticlockwise around the dance floor. It is characterised by the gliding motion of the dancers' feet and often involves the dancers rising and falling as a result of flexing their knees. A true Viennese waltz is danced at 6/8 time and with 180 beats per minute, and comprises just turns and change steps. Originally considered scandalous, it was the first social dance where people danced facing each other and close together, even if they were strangers. However, by 1816 it had become sufficiently acceptable that the Prince Regent allowed it at his society dances. What we know as the waltz is actually a slower development of the dance.

Aesthetics: examples are:

Slow waltz
Country western waltz
(dancers often in shadow position)
International waltz
(common competition style where dancers don't open out)
Viennese waltz

Dress: Although there's no strict dress code, clothes should be elegant, so flowing dresses and formal suits work well but don't forget your dance shoes! Each Viennese ball has its own dress code.

Did you know?

Chopin's 'Waltz in D Flat Major', Op 64 No 1, known as the 'Minute Waltz', actually lasts for more than 2 minutes. It is thought that the word 'minute' was originally used to describe its scale rather than its duration.

The Viennese ball season

Visit a Viennese ball and you'll be transported back to times of pure elegance and perfect manners. The events, with their wonderful customs, have been a tradition ever since Emperor Joseph II opened up his masked balls in the Hofburg Palace to the public. Although the world of waltz has changed in terms of strict etiquette, the Viennese ball still requires courtly behaviour, which includes no overtaking, a strict dress code, an opening fanfare, the entrance of the debutants and debutantes, dance calls, a quadrille and the formal ending. The season, which starts in November and peaks in January and February, attracts more than 3,000 visitors in more than 450 balls. That's more than 2,000 hours of dancing!

Foxtrot and quickstep

> *'Ballroom dancing is like being on Mars compared to what I've done throughout my life.'*
> JOEY MCINTYRE

What's it all about?

Diasporic dances with an American twist, the ever-popular foxtrot and quickstep share a common history and a similar style, although the former is more elegant and the latter more showy.

One theory as to how foxtrot came into being was that vaudeville entertainer Harry Fox set the trotting steps he used in his routine to the newly fashionable ragtime music in 1914. 'Fox's trot', which itself developed from other contemporary dances, turned into the foxtrot. Movements became much smoother, then slower, and the slow-quick-quick-slow steps we recognise today were born while the footwork still created a gliding action around the dance floor.

A faster-paced dance evolved at the same time as the modern-day foxtrot; this was the quickstep. While they were both initially performed to ragtime, dancing them to the big jazz bands of the late 1930s and 1940s became all the rage.

Aesthetics: Foxtrot, social foxtrot (a simpler version), quickstep.

Dress: Black tie and vintage clothes go down very well. Competition dresses tend to be mid-length to long and often very floaty, while the social dance code is more relaxed.

Did you know?

The oldest competitive ballroom dancer, Frederick Salta, passed his IDTA Gold Bar Level 3 examinations in Latin and ballroom with honours at the age of 100 years and 245 days, in Eltham, London, in October 2011. Among the ballroom dances he performed were the quickstep, tango and foxtrot.

Ballroom and Latin dance game changers

What is a dance game changer? It could be someone who changes the way things are done, or challenges conventions or transforms the accepted ways of doing things. It could be someone whose work makes you want to cry or sing or join in, or someone who gives you that little nudge that releases you into another world of understanding, or someone whose work introduced millions of people to a new idea. Here are some ballroom and Latin dance game changers.

Dancers

Harry Fox
1882–1959

In 1914, vaudeville dancer, actor and comedian Harry Fox (born Arthur Carringford) set the trotting steps he used in his routine to the newly fashionable ragtime music. These steps, known as 'Fox's trot' were recorded by dance instructor F. L. Clendenen in his 1914 book *Dance Mad*. Over time, as the steps themselves became smoother, the dance became known as the foxtrot.

Best known for: Giving his name to the foxtrot.

Anton du Beke
Born 1966

Cheeky chappie Anton du Beke is a ballroom dancer and TV presenter, best known for his long run as a professional competitor in the BBC's *Strictly Come Dancing* which he has taken part in since it began in 2004. He started dancing at the age of 14 at a local dance school in Sevenoaks, Kent, took his first dance exam in 1981 and entered his first competition a few years later.

Best known for: His *Strictly* persona, as a result of which he won the 2011 Rear of the Year award.

Best of the rest

Doris Lavelle (helped bring Latin dance to Europe with Monsieur Pierre)

Richard and Janet Gleave (champions eight times between 1973 and 1980)

Donnie Burns and Gaynor Fairweather (14 times pro-Latin champions).

Ballroom and Latin dance details

	Style	Music	Meter	Tempo (beats per minute)	Basic rhythm
Waltz	International standard (ballroom)	Slow ballads or instrumental music in 3/4 time.	3/4	84–90	123 123 (strong accent on 1)
Tango	International standard (ballroom)	Medium-tempo orchestral.	4/4	128–132	Quick-quick-slow
Viennese waltz	International standard (ballroom)	Fast music in 3/4 or 6/8 time, often classical, such as Strauss waltzes.	3/4 or 6/8	174–180	123 123 (strong accent on 1)
Slow foxtrot	International standard (ballroom)	Medium-slow jazz/swing music	4/4	112–120	Slow-quick-quick

Quickstep	International standard (ballroom)	Up-tempo jazz/swing music.	4/4	200–208	Slow-quick-quick
Cha-cha-cha	International Latin	Medium-tempo Latin music.	4/4	128	2, 3, 4&1, 2, 3, 4&1 (accent on 1)
Samba	International Latin	Medium tempo Brazilian–Latin music with strong downbeat.	2/4	100	1 a2 1 a2 (accent on downbeat)
Rumba	International Latin	Slow Latin ballad.	4/4	104	2 3 4 (1), 2 3 4 (1)
Paso doble	International Latin	Dramatic Latin 'bullfight' music; popular music is 'España Cañí'.	2/4	120–124	March
Jive	International Latin	Very fast swing music.	4/4	176	1 2, 3 a4, 3 a4
Waltz	American smooth (ballroom)	Slow ballads or instrumental music in 3/4 time.	3/4	84–96	123 123 (strong accent on 1)

Tango	American smooth (ballroom)	Medium-tempo orchestral.	4/4	120–128	Quick-quick-slow
Foxtrot	American smooth (ballroom)	Medium-tempo jazz/swing music.	4/4	120–136	Slow-quick-quick or slow-slow-quick-quick
Viennese waltz	American smooth (ballroom)	Fast music in 3/4 or 6/8 time.	3/4 or 6/8	162	123 123 (strong accent on 1)
Cha-cha	American rhythm	Medium-tempo Latin music.	4/4	112–120	2, 3, 4&1, 2, 3, 4&1 (accent on count 1)
Rumba	American rhythm	Medium-tempo Latin music.	4/4	128–144	Slow-quick-quick
East coast swing	American rhythm, social swing, country and Western	Fast swing music.	4/4	136–144	1 a2, 1 a2, 1 2 (accent on 2)
Bolero	American rhythm	Slow Latin ballad.	4/4	96–104	Slow-quick-quick
Mambo	American rhythm, social Latin	Up-tempo Latin music.	4/4	188–204	2 3 4 (1), 2 3 4 (1) Or 1 2 3 (4) 1 2 3 (4)

Choreographers and innovators

Victor Silvester
1900–78

Victor Marlborough Silvester OBE won the first World Ballroom Dancing Championships in 1922 with his partner Phyllis Clarke. He was a founding member of the Ballroom Committee of the ISTD (Imperial Society of Teachers of Dancing) which codified what the Americans call the 'international style' and published *Modern Ballroom Dancing*; the first book using the standards in 1927 (it has remained in print ever since). Sylvester had his own BBC TV show in the 1950s, was also a musician and bandleader who sold 75 million records between the 1930s and the 1980s and became president of the ISTD in 1945.

Best known for: The substantial influence he had on ballroom dance.

Best of the rest

Monsieur Pierre (Pierre Jean Philippe, instrumental in bringing ballroom and Latin dance to England)
Josephine Bradley (in 1934 influenced the slower foxtrot step)
Johann Strauss II (great waltz composer).

Principals, producers and directors

Eric Morley
1918–2000

Born in London, Eric Morley, who was orphaned at the age of 11, first understood the power of dance when he worked in entertainment at MECCA. In 1949 he introduced ballroom dancing to the BBC with *Come Dancing* and is indirectly responsible for the recent huge resurgence in the popularity of dance created by the *Strictly Come Dancing* series.

Best known for: Creating the Miss World pageants and bringing *Come Dancing* to the British public.

Best of the rest

Audrey Hepburn (waltzed in the film adaptation of Tolstoy's *War and Peace*)
Walter Laird (helped formalise Latin dancing).

Competitions

There is a range of organisations that provide and maintain the quality of their dance syllabus and a number of competitions, but there is really only one place that everyone dreams of competing. That is the eight-day Blackpool Dance Festival. The largest ballroom competition in the world, it has been running since 1920 and covers ballroom and Latin dancing, the British Open Championships, the Rising Star Amateur Ballroom and Latin Championships and the invitation-only Professional Team and Exhibition Competition.

Other competitions include the World Dance Championships of the WDC (World Dance Council), ISTD (Imperial Society of Teachers of Dancing) and the DanceSport associations, among others, each of which is hotly competitive and has its own rules.

Small and silver screens

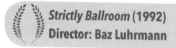

Strictly Ballroom (1992)
Director: Baz Luhrmann

Set in Australia, this drama tells the story of the fight of a young man with a domineering and conventional mother and a father who wishes he had the courage to have danced his own style in his day. The young man, who has the potential to win the Pan-Pacific Grand Prix Dancing Championship provided he does only what is expected of him, pairs up with a plain unknown dancer when his maverick style causes his regular partner to leave. They incorporate the paso doble into the dance (from the passionate side of her family), and the two compete in the Australian Pan Pacific Championships while staying true to their style.

Fascinating fact: Pretty much everything that could have provided a barrier to this film did; nobody wanted to finance it (even the first funder admits he'd never have funded it if he had only seen the script), the producer and a major actor died, nobody wanted to distribute it, but after it received a 15-minute ovation in Cannes there was a bidding war from the distributors and it won a string of international awards.

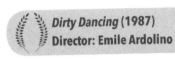

Dirty Dancing (1987)
Director: Emile Ardolino

Baby's hopes of enjoying her youth in the final summer before she plans to join the Peace Corps look to be dashed when she has to spend summer with her parents at a sleepy holiday camp in the Catskills. However, her luck changes when she meets dance instructor Johnny (Patrick Swayze), who teaches conservative dance steps to holidaymakers by day and heads to raucous dance parties at night. Johnny takes Baby as his dance partner and romance ensues.

Fascinating fact: Although Jennifer Grey and Patrick Swayze demonstrated their iconic lift at the audition, Grey was too scared to practice it and the only time she danced it was when she had to film the scene.

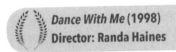

Dance With Me (1998)
Director: Randa Haines

After his mother passes away, young Cuban (Chayanne) goes to Houston to work as a handyman in a dance studio. It becomes clear that the owner of the studio, John Burnett (Kris Kristofferson) is the father he never knew. He decides to enter a local dance contest and falls for a dancer called Ruby (Vanessa L. Williams).

Fascinating fact: The film includes an homage to Gene Kelly when a sprinkler system turns on unexpectedly.

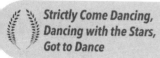

Strictly Come Dancing, Dancing with the Stars, Got to Dance

Whether celebrities and professional ballroom dancers fight it out in a ballroom dancing competition, regular people compete in a dance talent show or dancers show the world what they can do, TV reality shows all over the world have caused an enormous surge in the popularity of dancing.

Fascinating fact: Between 2004 and 2006, the dancers at *Strictly Come Dancing* used 169 bottles of fake tan (that's one bottle per couple per show), wore 330 costumes which used over three million sequins and went through 73 sets of false eyelashes.

CHAPTER 4

INDIAN DANCE

'Dance and music flow on to the canvas of the stage with the most unselfconscious brush strokes.'

SWAPNA SUNDARI

Indian dance is an inspirational type of practice. Whether venerable classical dances that can be traced back thousands of years, contemporary Indian ballet that experiments with the old dance traditions, the hundreds of thousands of folk dances or Bollywood, a new fusion of old disciplines with anything from anywhere that brings the right mood, there will be a dance form for you.

Indian classical and religious dance

What's it all about?

Hindu mythology has it that Brahmā (the Hindu god of creation) first conceived dance, and inspired the sage Bharata to write the Nātya Shastra, a description of sacred Hindu musical theatre styles that include guidelines which Indian classical dance must follow.

Historically classical dance was dedicated to worship (in temples), entertainment (for example at harvest time) or leisure (to celebrate special occasions) and often represented the major Hindu gods. However, as with all dance forms the function and classification of dance is blurred. Nowadays in modern India the reverse is also true. Deities can be invoked through religious folk dance forms and some classical dance forms – such as those that started in temples and royal courts – use hand gestures to retell episodes of mythological tales.

Aesthetics: There are a large number of classical and religious dance forms, each of which arose in different areas and for different reasons. A few of the main ones are:

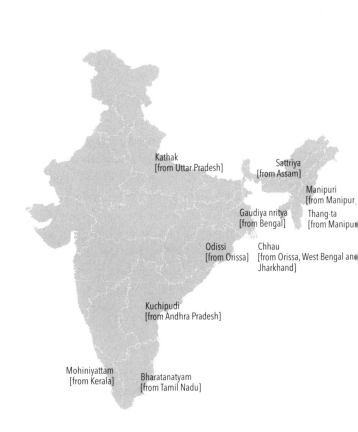

Kathak
[from Uttar Pradesh]

Sattriya
[from Assam]

Manipuri
[from Manipur]

Gaudiya nritya
[from Bengal]

Thang-ta
[from Manipur]

Odissi
[from Orissa]

Chhau
[from Orissa, West Bengal and Jharkhand]

Kuchipudi
[from Andhra Pradesh]

Mohiniyattam
[from Kerala]

Bharatanatyam
[from Tamil Nadu]

Dress: The dress for classical dance is as diverse as one would expect from such a huge continent. Colour codes are chosen based on the religion, ritual and dance concerned, and fine muslin and gold ornaments are often used. Ancient images show dancers and goddesses wearing a dhoti wrap, a predecessor to the modern sari.

Did you know?

Kathak and bharatanatyam dancers wear up to 200 bells to allow complex footwork to be heard by the audience. Beginners might start with 50 and build up as their skill increases.

Indian folk dance

There are hundreds, maybe thousands, of folk dances in India. Each state has its own folk dance forms, and most express the daily work and rituals of a community, have their roots in religious or seasonal festivals and are performed in groups. Most costumes are colourful and ornate, and contemporary folk dances have also integrated classical, folk and Western dance forms. Far simpler than the Indian classical dances, they have a minimum of steps and movements, and are more about joining in than doing the movements correctly. Some are performed by either men or women, while others are performed by both.

'The suggestive charm of bharatanatyam is forsaken
for overt narratives which play to the gallery. After
all… dance is… a community activity.'

LAKSHMI VISWANATHAN

Aesthetics:

Dumhal
[from Kashmir]

Bhangra
[from Punjab]

Sherdukpens
[from Arunachal Pradesh]

Bagurumba
[from Assam]

Matki dance
[from Madhya Pradesh]

Panthi
[from Chhattisgarh]

Kolattam
[from Andhra Pradesh]

Tarangamel
[from Goa]

Dress: While most costumes are flamboyant with lots of jewels, the details depend on the region concerned, for example Punjabi women wear a *ghagra choli* or a *lehenga choli* (embroidered short-sleeved blouses with long skirts) for their folk dances.

Did you know?

Bhangra was traditionally performed to celebrate the harvest.

Dance in film and entertainment

> 'Dance should always only suggest. Dance is always about the completion of the idea in the mind of the audience.'
>
> METHIL DEVIKA

After sound was introduced into cinema in India in the film *Alam Ara* in 1931, choreographed dance became almost mandatory in many Indian films. Hindi films use dance modelled on classical Indian dance styles, while modern films often blend dance styles together. Normally the hero and heroine dance a *pas de deux*, and another glamorous female figure performs a cameo. Dance choreographies are so popular that people at festivals, weddings and parties often perform a film choreography.

Mujra dancing

Creating a combination of exotic dance and art, the original mujra dancers were high-level courtesans who had learnt the art from their mothers. They performed for exalted patrons in the Mughal culture which traces its origins back to the Timurids and Genghis Khan. Mujra venues later became popular meeting places for those plotting the Indian Rebellion of 1857. Despite the integration of aspects of the dance form into modern-day Bollywood, its controversial past continues, as mujra clubs are all too often associated with prostitution.

Aesthetics: Mujra inherits complicated graceful arm movements from its kathak origins.

Interesting fact: Popular in Bollywood films, the movement called mujra is still the correct method of salutation with Maratha royal families.

Bollywood

'Bollywood stars are versatile; they not only act, but each one has the dance skills of John Travolta in Saturday Night Fever.*'*

CHRISTIAN LOUBOUTIN

Bollywood is a combination of the names Bombay (now called Mumbai) and Hollywood, and represents the largest film industry in the world. The highlights of Bollywood movies, which depict operatic and extravagant themes, are elaborate dance sequences performed to original soundtracks. It's not unusual to see a whole range of Indian and world dance styles in a Bollywood film, from slow descriptive movements to a high-energy fusion of traditional Indian forms with those of jazz, hip hop, belly dancing, Latin and even contemporary dance.

Aesthetics: The one consistent aspect is a perfectly coordinated choreography.

Interesting fact: Bollywood actors rarely sing the songs to which they dance.

Did you know?

The Nātya Shastra of Bharata, believed to have been created between 200 BC and AD 200, is the oldest surviving text on dance in the world. Some believe it was written by the sage Bharata, while others think it had various authors. It has been passed down orally through generations of hereditary actors, it covers all aspects of classical Sanskrit theatre and stagecraft. It is in the form of a dialogue between Bharata and a number of sages who approach him to ask about nātyaveda (the knowledge of performance and drama).

Indian dance game changers

Dancers

Thanjavur Balasaraswati
1918–84

From an unbroken lineage of musicians and dancers descended from those who served south India's eighteenth-century Thanjavur court, Thanjavur Balasaraswati was a dancer and singer in the south Indian karnatak tradition and one of the foremost experts of the bharatanatyam style of classical dance. From the 1960s she travelled the world and held residencies at a number of US institutions, training dancers and introducing new audiences to the art form.

Best known for: Being awarded the Padma Vibhushan, one of the country's top civilian honours, in 1977.

Best of the rest

Indian classical dance:	Bollywood:
Birju Maharaj	Hrithik Roshan
Indrani Rahman	Ranbir Kapoor
Sanjukta Panigrahi	Madhuri Dixit
Sitara Devi.	Urmila Matondkar
	Helen Jairag Richardson
	Amitabh Bachchan
	Aishwarya Rai.

Choreographers and innovators

Helen Jairag Richardson
Born 1938

Helen Jairag Richardson is of Anglo-Burmese descent and was a dancing megastar of Hindi films. What set her apart was the bold sensuous moves she used as part of the introduction of cabaret into Bollywood. She has appeared in more than 500 films and was herself the inspiration for four films and a book.

Best known for: Breaking the mould and blending cabaret into her Bollywood performances, she changed the portrayal of women from simple, sober and ethical, to sophisticated attractive people. She became the most popular film dancer of her times.

Best of the rest

Indian classical dance:	Mujra:
Natraj Gopi Krishna	Saima Khan
Akram Khan	Musarrat Shaheen.
Sonal Mansingh	
Uday Shankar.	

Principals, producers and directors

Born 1972

Born Ramesh Gopi, Remo D'Souza is an actor, dancer and choreographer-turned-director in the true Bollywood mode. His 3D movie *ABCD Any Body Can Dance* using winners of the first two seasons of *Dance India Dance* and two winners from *So You Think You Can Dance* was the first 3D Bollywood movie in a culture that rarely creates films that concentrate on just dance.

Best known for: Judging the *Strictly Come Dancing*-style reality show *Jhalak Dikhhla Jaa*.

Best of the rest

Indian classical dance:
Natraj Gopi Krishna
Mallikha Sarabai
Protima Gauri (Bedi).

Bollywood:
Govinda (Govind Arun Ahuja)
Shahid Kapoor
Aishwarya Rai
Vaijayanti Mala.

CHAPTER 5

JAZZ, SWING, STEP AND TAP

'Jazz has all the elements… it is the highest rendition of individual emotion.'
WYNTON MARSALIS

The fantastically flexible, expressive and joyful family of jazz dances have evolved from fusions of diasporic dances (particularly those from Africa), with rhythms, grooves and moves from the local American communities in which they were born. They caught on everywhere, and enthusiasts shared them all over the world as social dances.

Jazz dance

'Ginger Rogers did everything Fred Astaire did, except backwards and in high heels.'
BOB THAVES

What's it all about?

Jazz dance, which paralleled the development of jazz and was popularised by the big bands of the swing era, has developed myriad forms. Before the 1950s jazz dance referred to African American vernacular dance, a bent-kneed rhythmic improvisational dance (now often called traditional jazz). In the 1950s a new genre, with roots in Caribbean traditional dance emerged. Now called modern jazz (the foundation of this technique is turns, leaps, kicks and a fluid style), it is essentially an improvisational dance and everyone develops something unique. Jazz dance has had a huge impact on other dance forms since its inception and by the 1940s elements of jazz dance had reached the silver screen.

The slow drag (the dance for which ragtime music was composed that involves dragging alternate feet) of the nineteenth century influenced the cakewalk (an improvisational competitive square dance), which became a European ballroom craze and made way for social dances like the Charleston (1920s), the jitterbug (1930s and 1940s), the twist (1960s), disco dancing (1970s), fast foot shuffle, UK club jazz dance (1980s) and contemporary American solo jazz dance arose (which can be traced right back to when the first Africans were brought to US soil).

Aesthetics: Swing and its variations, UK jazz, popular jazz stage dance, jazz-influenced modern dance, eagle rock (nineteenth century), slow drag (nineteenth century).

Dress: Modern jazz dancers often wear soft leather shoes to help with sharp turns and twists. While anything goes, club jazz dancers favour period suits and trilby hats or black T-shirts and jeans, while stage performers and disco divas choose clothes with colours that reflect the energy of the dance.

> ### *Did you know?*
>
> *Jazz or tap dancers were considered an essential part of a jazz band in the early 1900s.*

Swing

'If you have to ask, you'll never know.'

LOUIS ARMSTRONG WHEN ASKED TO DEFINE THE RHYTHMIC CONCEPT OF SWING

What's it all about?

Energetic, happy, fun and athletic, swing encompasses a group of dances that developed with and from the swing style of jazz music from the 1920s to the 1950s and then on to the present day although the earliest swing dances predate the swing era. Swing jazz features the syncopated timing, bent knees and grounded moves associated with African American and West African music and dance. These partner dances evolved alongside the new big band jazz music produced in the late 1920s in places like Harlem, New York.

Swing evolved further as different cities drew on their own roots and cultural influences, combining them with other dance crazes and changing the staple African beats into a fast-paced, intricate groove. While legal constraints prevented socialising between African and white Americans, one of the main swing dance venues, the Savoy Ballroom, was very mixed.

During the 1980s swing dance re-emerged as various groups across the world decided to revive lindy hop by learning from the stars of the original swing era. This led to an increase in its popularity, including a huge revival in the UK, Sweden and the US.

'The only count I know is Count Basie.'

FRANKIE MANNING ON ANSWERING A QUESTION ABOUT COUNTS IN THE LINDY HOP

The shim sham

The shim sham, a series of moves that includes the double shuffle, the cross over and tack Annie (an up-and-back shuffle), is a wonderful example of why it is so difficult to categorise most dances. It was first improvised by Leonard Reed and Willie Bryant in the 1920s to be used as a quick finale. Easy to learn, they taught it to everyone in the show, so when one of the dancers (Joe Jones) was fired he went to New York, created a group and the group started doing the dance around Harlem, where it became known as the shim sham. The dance also evolved into a kind of ballroom dance without taps and, as it became more popular, dancers, singers and musicians would join together on stage at the end of a performance and finish the show with it. That's why similar dances with the same moves are considered to be tap dance's anthem by tap dancers and as a line dance that recalls the roots of swing by swing dancers.

Lindy hop, jitterbug and jive

> *'Wherever you go swing dancing everybody on the floor
> has one thing in common – a great big smile.'*
> SIMON SELMON

What's it all about?

It is said that in 1927, in New York's Savoy Ballroom, a reporter asked one of the dancers what dance was being performed. The enthusiast, named 'Shorty' George Snowden, who was reading about Charles Lindbergh's transatlantic flight to Paris, shortened part of the newspaper title he was reading 'Lindy hops to Paris' into 'lindy hop' and the name of the dance was born. Lindy hop, referred to as a happy dance, is known for its fast tempo, lifts, improvisation and rhythmical play, and is sometimes more than 300 beats per minute.

Jitterbug and lindy hops are essentially the same thing but different terms were used due to the cultural divisions of the times. American GIs brought the dance form to Europe and, with little or no formal teaching, the dance slowly changed. The big bands got smaller and the dancing evolved with the music, increasing the diversification of the dance throughout Europe. The UK transformed the dance into what we know today as jive and rock 'n' roll, Italy adopted the moniker boogie-woogie (although this is now a distinct style) and Sweden's jive dance became the buug.

Aesthetics: A true diasporic dance, swing also includes solo jazz routines such as the shim sham (originally created to bring everyone together at the end of a show), balboa and collegiate shag, French jive and ceroc (short for *c'est le roc*, it has no set footwork).

Dress: Anything goes, although many social swing dancers enjoy dressing in period clothes.

Did you know?

Jive talking was originally a kind of slang, then the word 'jive' became a derogatory epithet for less talented dancers. Nonetheless, the term stuck when the GIs brought the jitterbug to Europe during the Second World War.

Step dances

'Good tap dance is like a good sleight-of-hand – the feet are quicker than the eye.'
CHARLES 'HONI' COLES

Step dance is the term used for dances where the feet are the most important part of the routine, and where movements of upper body are either stylistically limited or mean much less than what is going on with the feet.

Aesthetics: Step dances have come into being all over the world and a few of the more esoteric are malambo (a rhythm-based dance from the Argentinian pampas danced by men in cowboy shoes), zapateado (a group of tap-like dances from Mexico) and stepping (an African American tradition where synchronised groups are led by a caller).

No tights, no tap

It is said that Ann Miller's costumes were so small and short that the dressers had to sew stockings to her briefs in order to cover her whole leg, making her one of the first women to wear pantyhose (tights)!

Irish dance

'If you feel like tapping your feet, tap your feet. If you feel like clapping your hands, clap your hands.'

ART BLAKEY

Danced solo or in groups, Irish step dance utilises two sorts of shoe depending on whether the sound is required for tap dancing or soft shoes for light-shoe dancing. Ireland's dance tradition can be traced all the way back to when the Celts brought dances to Ireland in 500 BC.

Aesthetics: Social dancing (which can be the formal four-person set dancing or the ceilidh where a caller leads the dance and everyone joins in), sean-nós (free-form dancing that is low to the ground and improvisational) and performance (which is usually an adaptation of the pure forms for stage).

Dress

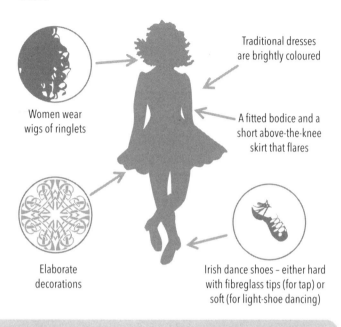

Women wear
wigs of ringlets

Traditional dresses
are brightly coloured

A fitted bodice and a
short above-the-knee
skirt that flares

Elaborate
decorations

Irish dance shoes – either hard
with fibreglass tips (for tap) or
soft (for light-shoe dancing)

Interesting fact: Each traditional Irish dance school has its own distinctive full-skirted dress, often featuring lace or embroidery of a pattern taken from the medieval Irish *Book of Kells*.

Did you know?

The largest number of people performing Irish dance in one place is 10,036 at the Dublin Irish Festival in Dublin Ohio, USA.

Tap dance

Tap dancing evolved in America as a fusion of the cultures and attitudes found there in the early nineteenth century. The melding of such different cultural disciplines, such as the jig, the African American juba dance, African drumming rhythms and various step dances including the Irish reel and Lancashire clog dance, gave rise to this unique percussive art.

Tap-dancing styles

Of the many comedy tap styles, legomania (also called rubber legs) incorporates high kicks and contortionist moves which can be seen danced by Ray Bolger's scarecrow performance to 'If I Only Had a Brain' in the 1939 film The Wizard of Oz.

Aesthetics: Over time tap dancers have created many styles and aesthetics which include:

Buck and wing

Ragtime (a solo dance in wooden shoes)

(a syncopated improvisational dance) Balletic tap

Clogging (which has a more flowing style)

(where heel and toe keep the rhythm) Tap

Flamenco

Dress: Tap-dancing shoes come in two types: those with metal plates on the toes and heels to make noise, and those with soft soles for soft-shoe dancing. Unless performing a story or thematic show, male tap dancers tend to wear jackets, waistcoats and fitted trousers, while women wear knee-length skirts.

Did you know?

Known as 'the littlest tap dancer in Hollywood', Shirley Temple could out-dance any adult from when she was seven to ten years old. Temple and Bill 'Bojangles' Robinson (a huge influence on the child star) performed many dances together, often traversing a set of stairs while displaying their intricate moves.

Step dance game changers

There's something romantic about step and tap-dancing hoofers. Maybe it's their association with the golden era of film or that old black-and-white film footage adds a retrospective glamour to an era that seems particularly glamorous already. Maybe it's just that the dances attract talented individuals who are so totally committed to their work that they can't fail to entrance anyone else who's exposed to it too.

Dancers

Fred Astaire and Ginger Rogers
1899–1987 and 1911–95

The famous American duo, both singers and actors, stole the hearts of millions with their special signature blend of tap and ballroom moves. Fred Astaire, who was also a musician and choreographer, had a stage, film and television career spanning 76 years and 31 musical films; while Oscar-winning Ginger Rogers was in 70 movies and had a penchant for art.

Best known for: Their musical comedies.

The Nicholas Brothers
Fayard Antonio Nicholas – 1914–2006
Harold Lloyd Nicholas – 1921–2000

The Nicholas Brothers were considered by many to be the greatest dancers of their day. They had grown up surrounded by vaudeville acts and became jazz circuit stars with their intricate, athletic song-and-dance routines in the early 1930s. By the start of the 1940s the pair were international celebrities with a number of successful film appearances.

Best known for: Mixing tap with acrobatics.

25th May

Bill 'Bojangles' Robinson
1878–49

Robinson began his career in minstrel revues, where both black and white men imitated slave dancing, and went on to be America's most famous tap dancer. He danced on Broadway in the 1920s and found success in Hollywood, where he appeared with child star Shirley Temple, becoming the most highly paid black American actor in the early twentieth century.

Best known for: His birthday, 25 May, which is now America's National Tap Dance Day.

Best of the rest

Eleanor Powell (exuberant tap dancer actress)
Michael Flatley (*Riverdance*)
Jean Butler (*Riverdance* and the Irish step)
Colin Dunne (actor and dancer)
Gregory Hines (dancer and actor)
Ruby Keeler (tap dancer, singer and actor)
Ann Miller (who once had the world's fastest feet)
Sammy Davis Jr (entertainer, dancer and singer).

Choreographers and innovators

Gene Kelly
1912–96

Athletic, energetic, ebullient American dancer, actor, singer, film director, producer and choreographer, Eugene Curran 'Gene' Kelly blended tap with balletic and athletic moves. He was the first person who wanted to choreograph both dance and cameras, to make something that could only be done on screen. That meant he had to choreograph the cameras in relation to the dance numbers as well as the dances themselves!

Best known for: *Singin' in the Rain*

Savion Glover
Born 1973

American Savion Glover is an award-winning tap dancer, actor, teacher and choreographer who is credited with the 1980s tap revival. A young prodigy who performed in *The Tap Dance Kid* on Broadway when he was 12, he was taught by famous dancers including Gregory Hines. His style is funky and sharp, and takes tap back to its African roots. He also won a choreography Tony Award for *Bring in 'da Noise, Bring in 'da Funk*.

Best known for: 'Hitting', which means communicating through his steps.

Best of the rest

Lester Horton (imitated Native American dance)
Jack Cole (the father of theatrical jazz dance)
Irene and Vernon Castle (initiated many modern jazz forms)
Frankie Manning (whose style of dance evolved into lindy hop).

Principals, producers and directors

Bob Fosse
1927–87

Robert Louis 'Bob' Fosse was an American dancer, actor, choreographer and director, and had considerable influence on the dance world. His dance style was cool, entertaining and joked with the audience. He loved the 'jazz hands' move and bucked convention, dancing with hips forward instead of back, and with his knees bent and slightly turned in. He didn't like losing his hair or his hands so he wore hats and gloves. He won eight Tony Awards for choreography and one for direction.

Best known for: His huge body of work and distinctive style that influenced many dancers including Michael Jackson.

Busby Berkeley
1895–1976

Musical choreographer Busby Berkeley became a movie director because he was unhappy with the limited role given to dance directors in Hollywood. With his signature use of one-camera close-ups, he created some of the biggest Hollywood dance spectaculars with sophisticated geometric patterns shot from amazing bird's-eye angles. He created the dance for *42nd Street*. Berkeley worked with a number of stars and eventually directed a different style of musical such as *Take Me Out to the Ball Game* with newcomer Gene Kelly.

Best known for: Never having had a dance lesson and being terrified that people might find out. He also had a knack of driving his producers crazy when he'd give orders to build a set, then sit in front of it for days, thinking up the choreography.

Best of the rest

Katherine Dunham (educator, documenter and social activist)
William Henry 'Juba' Lane (created tap dance as we know it).

The small and silver screen

Jazz, swing, step and tap have been taking the small and silver screen by storm for years. Guaranteed to entertain, whether from the glitz and glam of the stage or the hustle and bustle of smoky bars, these films are just some of the favourites out there.

42nd Street (1933)
Director: Lloyd Bacon

Broadway director Julian Marsh (Warner Baxter) tries to revive flagging fortunes with an ambitious musical. His leading lady Dorothy Brock (Bebe Daniels) is torn between the show's wealthy backer Abner Dillon (Guy Kibbee) and penniless actor Pat Denning (George Brent), and aspiring young Peggy Sawyer (Ruby Keeler) is hoping for her big break. This show within a show is a story of hard work and perseverance paying off when a talented understudy gets a chance to perform.

Fascinating fact: Filmed during the Great Depression.

All That Jazz (1979)
Director: Bob Fosse

Addicted to work, drugs and sex, Joe Gideon (Roy Scheider) finds it hard to simultaneously balance working on a Broadway musical and a Hollywood film and ends up hospitalised. His dream sequences are filled with glittering dance arrangements and the finale shows him centre stage.

Fascinating fact: Fosse survived a heart attack shortly before his new film idea which tells a story with obvious autobiographical links.

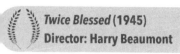

Twice Blessed (1945)
Director: Harry Beaumont

Two blonde identical twins (played by Lee and Lyn Wilde) have been apart since the divorce of their parents seven years ago. Each envies the other's lifestyle so they agree to swap places for a few days. Hilarity ensues as they realise that changing lives is not so easy but agree to continue when they realise it might help get their parents back together. This film, a precursor to 1961's *The Parent Trap* includes some wonderful lindy hop and swing.

Fascinating fact: This was a vehicle for The Wilde Twins who are still alive and in their 90s.

Singin' in the Rain (1952)
Directors: Stanley Donen and Gene Kelly

Don Lockwood (Gene Kelly) is forced to change his film from silent to musical and has to find a voice extra, as his leading lady Lina Lamont (Jean Hagen)'s voice is horrible. His best friend Cosmo Brown (Donald O'Connor) suggests Kathy Selden (Debbie Reynolds) and a muddle ensues. This film contains some of the best-loved dance numbers in musical history.

Fascinating fact: The musical has very little original music and the writers had to write the plot to fit what was available.

West Side Story (1957)
Directors: Jerome Robbins and Robert Wise

A modern-day *Romeo and Juliet* set in New York, *West Side Story* is a tale of romance amid street gang rivalry. The story, which was originally a musical, was adapted for the screen in 1961, with music by Leonard Bernstein and choreographies by Jerome Robbins.

Fascinating fact: While shooting the famous prologue on the streets of Manhattan, the performers sustained mild injuries from dancing and leaping on the hard concrete and were harassed by locals. Ironically, the film-makers ended up having to hire a street gang to protect them.

Hellzapoppin' (1941)
Director: H. C. Potter

A fast, furiously funny and chaotic romantic comedy based on the Broadway hit of the same name, this film features two friends trying to turn their musical show into a movie. Gags and dance numbers abound along with references to other films of the period.

Fascinating fact: When Universal originally optioned *Hellzapoppin'* the idea was to film the play as it was; an improvisational comedy review with zany props, no story and no two performances exactly the same but they got cold feet and superimposed both romance and plot.

CHAPTER 6

SPANISH AND LATIN DANCE

'Master technique and then forget about it and be natural.'
ANNA PAVLOVA

Spanish and Latin dances are united by the common aesthetics of original Spanish dance, which was taken to Latin America by Spanish conquerors and subsequent settlers; while flamenco, whose history only started to be documented over the past 200 years, derived from the flamenco song, which coupled a primitive cry or chant with a rhythm made by feet stomping on the floor. Born from passionate, lively and provocative cultures, these dances promise a performance that is intoxicating and compelling to watch.

Spanish dance and flamenco

'What makes flamenco goes back more than 800 years, from the culture left by the Arabs, the Jewish influences and indigenous creativity. It is written that people were imported from Cádiz to entertain aristocracy 3,500 years ago, so flamenco draws from a huge tradition.'
PACO PEÑA

As far as it's possible to classify the dances of an entire country, Spanish dance can be divided into four major groups: flamenco, escuela bolera, neoclassical dance and regional dances, which can be further divided into court and religious dances. Flamenco was originally passed down through the generations, while escuela bolera, considered Spain's national dance in the nineteenth century, has a more academic tradition. Consider that there are around 200 regional dances from the Catalan region alone and you'll get a feel of how many there are in the entire country, throughout which even the castanets are played in different ways.

Honoured for the preservation of Spanish dance

In 1989 Dame Marina Keet was honoured by King Juan Carlos I for her presentation and preservation of Spanish dance, and received the Carina Ari medal from Princess Christina of Sweden for her contribution to ballet in Sweden. Dame Marina is co-founder of the Spanish Dance Society, the largest society in the world dedicated to the advancement of Spanish dance in all its forms.

Flamenco

With its history shrouded in mystery, what we recognise as flamenco probably resulted from the fusion of the two proud cultures of Andalusian Spain and that of the *Gitanos* (Romanies) who arrived as a result of the great Indian diaspora and expressed their marginalisation and the way they missed their homelands through music and dance. As the *Gitanos'* predecessors travelled, their ancient sacred Hindu dances were influenced by Greeks, Romans, Egyptians and more. Duende, the essence of flamenco, is a quality of experience that links audience and performers, reminding all of flamenco's roots and the joy and pain that it expresses.

Aesthetics: The family tree of flamenco includes soleá (a frenetic angular dance originally performed by women) considered the mother of flamenco and one of the oldest *palos* (music compositions), bulerías (based on a similar rhythm to the soleá but much faster) and alegrías (meaning 'joys'). This is one of the strictest dances in terms of format, it has five different sections.

Dress: Traditionally women have worn long dresses, often with ruffles and the *bata de cola* (flamenco skirt with long tail) and men often wore high-waisted trousers. Nowadays they sometimes swap. Other dance forms require the *manton* (scarf), *sombrero* (hat), *peineta* (hair comb) and *abaniko* (fan).

Did you know?

A heated debate about whether flamenco should remain pure or integrate other influences has existed for as long as records exist. However, nowadays many dancers combine both happily, even learning other dance forms to provide a different perspective to their pure flamenco.

The jota

What's it all about?

Originating from Aragon, northern Spain, in the 1700s, the name itself comes from the Latin word for 'jump'. This Spanish folk dance combines song and music to a lively partner dance in fast 3/4 or 4/8 time. As it spread through the regions of Spain, the style and tempo of the dance inevitably changed into variations of the original, some of which are from the regions of Catalonia, Castile, Navarra, Cantabria, Asturias, Galicia, La Rioja, Murcia and eastern Andalusia.

Aesthetics: Although there is too much variation between the regional dances to give specifics, the jota has a similar feel to the waltz, but with much freer movements and a more informal atmosphere. The music and song also play a big part in creating the overall performance and differ from region to region, for example the Castilian style is accompanied by guitars, bandurrias, lutes, dulzainas and drums, while the Galicians use bagpipes, drums and bombos.

Dress: Women's clothing tends to have shorter over-the-knee skirts while men often wear pantaloons with laced shoes.

> ### Did you know?
> *Legend has it that the jota was brought north from Andalusia by the exiled Moorish poet Aben Jot.*

The sardana

What's it all about?

Danced in the Catalan area of both Spain and France, this traditional regional folk dance is a circle dance to 6/8 rhythm where the leader communicates by squeezing hands. Everyone is welcome to join in and there is no sense of exclusiveness. Once one circle becomes too crowded smaller circles start to emerge to accommodate both adults and children. Although its origins aren't clear, it was well known in the sixteenth century. Italian operas have increased its popularity and the dance is identified with Catalan values of brotherhood, harmony and democracy.

> ### Did you know?
> *You can see the sardana every Sunday outside Barcelona's La Seu cathedral and along the coast.*

Aesthetics: The sardana is usually broken into two sections: curts and llargs, which can be repeated however many times to create a pattern of movement. Participants lower their arms when performing the curts section and then raise them to shoulder height when doing the llargs. The footwork varies from one region to the next but is consistent in that it is intricate and light.

Dress: This is a social dance that people join on the way back from church or just because they come across an event when they've gone for a walk, so most people dress as they would anywhere else. However the sardana was traditionally danced in *espardenya*, a type of footwear similar to espadrilles made of esparto grass fabric and with two long fabric strips to tie them up around the ankle.

Did you know?

Sardana game changer Joseph Vidalon has been responsible for much of the recording and curating of the sardana's history and documents which can still be seen in the official Sardana Society offices in a village in the foothills of French Catalonia.

Latin dances

'The philosopher's soul dwells in his head… the soul of the dancer abides in all her body.'

KHALIL GIBRAN

Latin dances are a fusion of dance moves that originated in Latin America, with influences from different countries, such as Africa, Spain and Portugal. It's possible to trace many of the dances' steps and techniques, for example the movement where a pair breaks away and continues to dance without touching is thought to derive from European ballroom dance.

Social Latin dance forms, including salsa, samba, mambo, danzón, lambada and merengue, have inspired similar ballroom dance forms. Ballroom codification has also resulted in formalised Latin dances such as the cha-cha-cha, rumba, samba, paso doble and jive.

Aesthetics: There are hundreds of variations of Latin dances, many of which have become popular throughout the world. Son is a Cuban dance to Spanish guitar and Bantu (African) instruments; paso doble is a competition dance modelled on bullfights; lambada involves a sideways rhythmic movement; and the much older merengue is based on Dominican Republican folk dances.

Dress: Social and club dancers' dress style depends entirely on the environment, while Latin costumes for balls and competitions are designed to be bright, eye-catching and colourful. Ladies' dresses are short and men's shirts often sparkly.

Did you know?

Pérez Prado is the musician credited with creating the first mambo and encouraged dancers to perform as part of the set.

Cha-cha-cha

> 'Taking a step backward after taking a step
> forward is not a disaster, it's a cha-cha.'
> ROBERT BRAULT

What's it all about?

With origins traced from the danzón, which evolved from the Cuban habanera, a genre of popular Cuban music influenced by a fusion of African rhythmic and popular European dance styles, the cha-cha-cha takes its name from the music's very distinctive rhythm and the way the footwork reflects this with intricate shuffles. Western countries came to know about this genre when Monsieur Pierre travelled from London to Cuba to study their style of dance. On learning the technique he started teaching it in the UK.

Aesthetics: There are three styles in cha-cha-cha, all of which are variants of the original. Ballroom and social are similar, but differ in the chasse movement (the cha-cha-cha) as one travels sideways using up all the space and the other is performed forwards and backwards in a much tighter space, respectively. International Latin and American rhythm are performed at a competitive level.

Dress: Short and swinging dresses, tight men's clothes often with sparkles.

Rumba

'Dance, my darling dance! If you dance then death can't catch you! Nothing bad can touch you! Dance!'
JACKIE FRENCH, LADY DANCE

What's it all about?

A dance thought to have evolved from the Cuban dance the bolero-son and influenced by Spanish and African dance, rumba, which is also the word for 'party', comprises accentuated hip movements to a slow, sensuous controlled beat. Ballroom rumba is not to be confused with Afro-Cuban rumbas, which often take the shorthand form 'rumba', as they are very different types of dance. Considered the sexiest of the five Latin-American ballroom dances, rumba tells a story of love, passion and excitement between the dancers through swaying motions, sharp eye contact and intimate body language.

Aesthetics:

Cuban rumba
International ballroom rumba
Flamenco rumba
American-style ballroom rumba
African rumba
Catalan rumba
(folkloric dance unrelated to Cuban rumba)

Dress: Short and swinging dresses, tight men's clothes often with sparkles; traditionally the woman would wear a skirt with a long ruffled train made out of hens' feathers, while the man's ruffled shirt sleeves would be made from cocks' feathers to distinguish their roles.

Did you know?

Flamenco rumba is different from Cuban rumba, having evolved from dance to cantes de ida y vuelta (literally 'round-trip songs': music that has travelled to and evolved a little in Latin America before coming back and evolving further in Spain), while African rumba is different again, having evolved from dances to Congolese music.

Samba

> *'Our revolution is the joy of samba.'*
> ALEXANDRE LOUZADA

What's it all about?

Emblematic of Brazilian identity, the samba has arisen from a fusion of native Brazilian, African (particularly Angolan and Congolese) and Portuguese cultures. Samba, which is danced socially on the streets during Carnival in the days before Lent, first reached the US in the 1920s. Ballroom samba requires a bouncy action, fast footwork and a lot of travelling around the dance floor.

Aesthetics: Different styles of samba have evolved throughout Brazil and in different districts of Rio de Janeiro.

Dress: While the dress code in ballroom samba is similar to the dress code for other Latin dances, samba dancers at Carnival wear clothes that show their bodies to the best effect, often with sequined bras and enormous headdresses with beautiful feathers and glitter. Male samba dancers also bear a lot of skin and wear brightly coloured costumes.

Did you know?

Samba de roda, which is the main root of the samba performed in Rio, was formally recognised as a UNESCO Heritage of Humanity dance in 2005.

Salsa

'I dance like I have a chip on my shoulder. I dance salsa.'
JAROD KINTZ

What's it all about?

A sexy and romantic diasporic dance, salsa has continued to evolve and now elements of jazz dance and rock are often combined with its trademark side-to-side moves. Popular all over the world with social, amateur and professional dancers, salsa arose from a fusion of Latin and Afro-Caribbean dance styles in the 1900s. It is most commonly danced on an eight-beat pattern (two bars of four) where the steps are impeccably timed with the music, giving the dance its fast, upbeat characteristics. The male dancer usually leads his partner's moves but the effort isn't taken away from the woman who must keep on time and balanced throughout the performance.

Aesthetics: The large number of salsa styles include Cuban style or casino, which depicts a sensual and flirtatious partner dance; Cuban suelto (solo dance); Rueda de casino, a style where dancers swap partners throughout the performance; Puerto Rican; New York, developed in the 1970s and 1980s and becoming more popular, favouring shines over spins and turns; Cali, one of the fastest styles which combines super intricate footwork and tight spins while remaining close to the partner; and Miami, a style which is centred on shines and show-offs.

Dress: Women wear sequinned-bikini dresses that show off the figure and accentuate the breasts and hips. The dresses cut off at knee-length or higher for freer movement and 4-inch heels are worn. The costumes tend to be dark, such as reds and blacks to hide marks and emphasise the sequin patterns. Men wear stretchy but well-fitted black trousers, a flamboyant V-neck shirt, which often has lace to show off their lean body, and smart shoes. The man's costume is always more modest so that the attention of the audience is drawn to the woman.

Did you know?

Some people say that the wave-like movement of salsa dancers represents the water over which slaves were transported, while others can trace the movement back to original African dances.

Mambo

'A day I don't dance is a day I don't live.'
ANONYMOUS

What's it all about?

Mambo, which has its roots in big-band American jazz and the rumba, was particularly popular in the 1950s. It was formally established by Pérez Prado in Cuba, who later popularised the dance in Mexico. However, the mambo known to Cubans and Mexicans evolved into a more disciplined style when it hit New York, as American professional dancers felt it was too extreme and needed to be standardised for the social and ballroom market. The ballroom mambo's distinctive moves are rock steps and side kicks, while the hips create the literal mambo, which means 'shake it' in the argot of the Cuban sugar cane hackers.

Aesthetics: Modern mambo is danced to both mambo and salsa dura (old-school salsa), while danzón is considered by some to be both source and original mambo.

Did you know?

The 1992 film Mambo Kings *starring Armand Assante and Antonio Banderas was based on a novel called* The Mambo Kings Play Songs of Love *by Oscar Hijuelos.*

Tango

'Tango is the most profound dance in the history of the world.'
WALDO EMERSON

What's it all about?

While the exact origins of tango are shrouded in mystery, it is known that, by the time Argentina banned slavery in 1853, the word tango was used by ex-slaves as meaning 'a place to dance'. However, the dance we now know didn't form until the early 1900s when the ports of Buenos Aires and Montevideo had become a melting pot of cultures; a result of people travelling to Latin America to seek a living. African, Spanish, Italian, British, Polish, Russian and native-born Uruguayans and Argentinians mixed up their music and dance, and from this tango was born.

In this immigrant society a man could only get close to a woman through prostitution or dance, so there was fierce competition between men on the dance floor, and if a woman didn't enjoy dancing with someone she'd tell her friends, so men started practising together (which attracted more men for other reasons too), and the music and dance became the unifying aspect between cultures. The only place live music was available was at brothels, and this is where the Argentinian upper classes first encountered the dance, although it only became popular in Argentina after the craze hit France, Europe and the US.

Aesthetics: There are various different tangos, the most popular of which are Argentinian tango, ballroom tango and Finnish tango. Ballroom tango has fixed steps and a formal style with partners arching away from each other in their upper bodies (in competition they're not allowed to break their close hold). Argentinian tango, which is more improvised and closer to the original style, has straight bodies that keep their own balance but appear to lean towards each other. Finnish tango combines the improvisational aspects of Argentinian tango with the rhythms and timing of ballroom tango, although Finns have been composing their own tango music for decades.

Dress: Competitive ballroom tango dresses are currently knee length, American smooth dresses have split skirts and social tango tends to be much more casual. In Buenos Aires people dancing social tango wear nice knee length dresses but it's considered poor taste to be too flashy.

> ### *Did you know?*
>
> *Al Pacino learned to dance tango in a New York dance studio for the film* Scent of a Woman.

Spanish and Latin dance game changers

The passion, fire and energy required by those involved in Latin dance is very demanding, and many game changers work directly with the dance. However, as with other dance forms credit should also be given to musicians such as Tito Puente, Carlos Gardel and Astor Piazzolla, who revolutionised mambo, popularised and revolutionised tango music, respectively, thereby causing a resurgence in interest in the dances.

Other major game changers are Francisco Vazquez who created LA-style salsa; Shayene Cesário who was Rio's 2010 Carnival Queen and later Queen of Estácio de Sá Samba School (arguably the top samba school in Brazil); Johnny Vazquez, who won the Mayan World Salsa Championships several times; Olavo Alén who danced the first rumba; Monsieur Pierre (Pierre Zurcher-Margolle), who developed and codified the current ballroom style cha-cha-cha; Pablo Veron, who is considered the link between new and old styles of tango; Miguel Angel Zotto, who is known for the spectacular sets and excellent choreography of his troupe.

Flamenco game changers

> *'If I know some twenty distinct definitions of flamenco,*
> *it is because I have asked that many aficionados to*
> *express the meaning of the art they love. I could have*
> *enjoyed thirty definitions if I had bothered to ask ten others.'*
>
> KEN HAAS

While they have all held the same passion for flamenco, each of these people, both in the past and present, have brought different things to the art. There's not even a hint of similarity in the incredible amalgam of styles with which they dance, whether or not they're influenced by other flamencos or came to the dance from a different tradition, such as that of classical or contemporary dance.

Dancers

Pastora Imperio
1887–1979

This *cantaor* (singer) and dancer with a repertoire extending to other Spanish traditions – such as the country's folk dances and Spanish classical dance – contributed a form of 'majesty' to her dance, particularly in the technique of twisting arms and waist.

Best known for: Developing the female dance technique.

Carmen Amaya
1918–63

The most extraordinary personality of all time in flamenco dance, Carmen Amaya started performing in waterfront bars in Barcelona when she was five years old and revolutionised women's *zapateo* (footwork). The musician Sabicas, who later accompanied her, said that her dancing seemed supernatural. She took a rootsy style of flamenco to American theatres and both she and El Gran Antonio were the first to appear in flamenco dance films such as *Queen of the Gypsies*.

Best known for: Taking flamenco back to Barcelona.

Best of the rest

Joaquin Cortés
Rafaela Carrasco
Belén Maya
La Argentina
Pilar Lopez.

Choreographers and innovators

Antonio Gadés
1936–2004

Gadés revolutionised the international flamenco scene through his own elegant dance style and collaborations with film-maker Carlos Saura. He took flamenco *obras* (works) to a new level of sophistication and his trilogy of films with Saura and Cristina Hoyos opened flamenco up to new audiences all over the world.

Best known for: His enduring choreographies.

Israel Galván and Enrique Morente
Born 1973 and 1942–2010

Rubén Olmo, director of Ballet Flamenco de Andalucia says that Israel Galván is 'without doubt the most influential in the panorama of flamenco dance, for his valour, staying true to his style despite initial rejection'. Once rejected for his determined reconstructions and incorporation of themes including Spanish danza into elaborate and complicated moves, he has now achieved the status of flamenco superstar.

Galván himself believes Enrique Morente to have had the most influence. This controversial singer, who plunged into experimentalism while staying true to his roots, was also once resisted, but is now considered as having started a tradition of his own.

Best known for: Sticking to controversial ideas despite opposition until they became respected artists with a huge following.

Eva Yerbabuena
Born 1970

Eva Yerbabuena changed the concept of performance through applying her knowledge of the female body to develop a whole different range of authentic flamenco techniques. Her staging and concepts are staggering and the integration with the music is phenomenal. This moves us away from the *tablao* (traditional flamenco stage) to fantastic modern productions that are brilliantly conceived.

Best known for: Her early pure flamenco performances.

Best of the Rest

Olavo Alén (documented rumba)
Francisco Vazquez (originator of LA-style salsa).

Principals, producers and directors

Federico García Lorca
1898–1936

This great flamenco enthusiast worked with Manuel de Falla to reinstate *cante jondo* (a vocal style in flamenco) in a competition in 1922. Lorca's influence is profound; it romanticised the art form and his 1933 study on the aesthetics of *duende* (the visceral feeling transferred by performance) remains the seminal work of its kind.

Best known for: His writings, some of which, such as *Bodas de Sangre* (*Blood Wedding*) have been made into flamenco films by a number of well-known producers.

Best of the rest

Carlos Saura (film producer)

Manolo Caracol (although a singer he opened the most famous tablao in Madrid in 1959)

General Franco (politician, whose government brought new flamenco clubs along the Costa del Sol upon realising that flamenco was a potential tourist moneymaker)

Cristina Hoyos (dancer, for extending flamenco's international reach by performing in the 1992 Summer Olympics and the creation of the world's first flamenco dance museum)

Joseph Vidalon (president of French Sardanas Association).

Did you know?

Of all the popular dances, flamenco and bharatanatyam are the only two where dance and music form an equal partnership. Rhythmic signals from the dancers instruct the musicians in the same way a change of verse might instruct the dancer to perform the next part of a choreography.

'His triumph was the flamenco. Sir, what a dance! What tragedy!'

Pierre Louÿs, *La Femme et le Pantin*

Small and silver screens

 ***Bodas de Sangre (Blood Wedding)* (1981), *Carmen* (1983) and *El Amor Brujo (Love the Magician)* (1986)**
Director: Carlos Saura

A choreographer and lead dancer is interviewed while a dance troupe gathers backstage to tell the tragic tale of romance and doom in a flamenco interpretation of Federico Garcia Lorca's play *Blood Wedding*. As the group of flamenco dancers rehearses their version of *Carmen* the choreographer falls in love with the dancer acting as Carmen and the two stories blend.

Fascinating fact: Saura began his film career directing controversial political films about Spanish dictator Francisco Franco, but transitioned into producing flamenco-dance dramas after the politician's death.

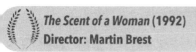

The Scent of a Woman (1992)
Director: Martin Brest

A preparatory school student takes a job as an assistant to irascible blind retired army officer Lieutenant Colonel Frank Slade (Al Pacino). One of the most captivating scenes in the film is when Slade tangos with a beautiful woman named Donna (Gabrielle Anwar) who enthralls him.

Fascinating fact: Professional ballroom dancer Paul Pellicoro choreographed the famous tango scene.

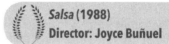

Salsa (1988)
Director: Joyce Buñuel

Rémi Bonnet (Vincent Lecoeur), brilliant pianist, abandons classical music to pursue his real musical passion, salsa. He heads for Paris but is unable to find work as himself so he pretends to be a Latin immigrant. He gets a job giving dance lessons to the locals, and meets and falls in love with Nathalie (Christianne Gout) with the inevitable result.

Fascinating fact: Joyce Buñuel is the daughter-in-law of legendary filmmaker Luis Buñuel.

CHAPTER 7

URBAN AND STREET DANCE

'Dance is infinite.'
STORM, BATTLE SQUAD

What's it all about?

Street dance (which used to be called vernacular dance) is any dance style that evolved outside a dance studio or school, be it the streets, alleyways, dance parties, parks, bandstands, school yards, raves and nightclubs. Old-style street dances, which include locking, popping, breaking, waacking and voguing, have specific styles and rules while new-style 'street' combines old movements but is much more flexible in terms of its rules.

Aesthetics: there are thousands, including:

Argentinian tango
The gumboot dance **Breaking**
The Melbourne shuffle
Flamenco (an Australian rave dance)
Liquiding **House** Capoeira
(a gestural dance to electronic music)
Clowning **Punk rock** Waacking
Krumping Samba
Voguing Freestyle

Dress: Because urban and street dances are such vast genres and span generations as well as most of the world, different strands of the dance form have their own distinct looks which match the trends of the times they originated from, for example old-style is associated with nylon tracksuits and high-top trainers, a reflection of the New York street fashion in the 1970s.

Did you know?

Freestyle is about an individual dancer's interpretation of the music. It should not be planned, has to be of and in the moment and once you've mastered the basics, musicality and rhythm is what matters.

Hip hop

What's it all about?

A cohesive term for breaking, popping and locking that didn't arise until after the individual dance forms, hip hop refers to street dance and urban styles that include breaking, locking and popping. Hip hop culture is considered to be a way of life and includes certain graffiti styles, dance battles and social dance, with an inclusiveness extended to people young and old.

Hip hop started on the street and people continue to learn from each other in public. Breakers still practice on cardboard on the pavement and there are often unofficial spots where they congregate. London's Royal Festival Hall has acknowledged this to such an extent that they issue timetables so that young dancers know when they can practice indoors. You can see them every month when dancer and choreographer Sean Graham (creator of CSDC, the Collective Solutions Dance Consortium, a loose collective of all dancers who use the facilities) posts the new timetable on Facebook.

Did you know?

Clogging (a folk dance using wooden shoes where the rhythm is marked by striking heels and toes on the floor) is sometimes considered the first street dance because it evolved in urban environments during the Industrial Revolution (between 1760 and 1840).

Hip hop: a brief history

Early 1970s DJ Kool Herc uses two turntables to extend the instrumental part of records at Bronx block parties. Don Campbell creates dance group The Lockers, originally named The Campbell Lockers.

1971 The TV show *Soul Train* is first aired.

1972 James Brown's hit 'Get on the Good Foot' causes the Good Foot dance craze.

1978 The Electric Boogaloos, the street dance group that made popping and boogaloo widespread, forms.

1983 The film *Wild Style*, based on hip hop culture and flash dancing, is the first mainstream film to feature breakdance.

Mid-1970s Disco dance becomes a standard in nightclubs in Europe and the US.

Mid-1970s House music in Chicago and New York continues to get more popular.

1990s Organised battle events, including Battle of the Year (Germany), B-Boy Summit and Freestyle Session (USA), B-Boy Championships (UK), The Notorious IBE (Holland) and Juste Debout (France), become increasingly popular.

Early 1990s Thomas Johnson, AKA Tommy the Clown, creates the style of dance known as clowning when performing at birthday parties.

2005 David LaChapelle's film *Rize* tells the story of clowning and krumping.

2005-06 *Step Up*, starring Channing Tatum, is released and is later followed by four sequels.

2006 Salah wins reality dance TV show *Incroyable Talent* (France).

2007 The film *Planet B-Boy* tells the history of breaking.

2007 The House Dance International festival is established in New York City. It celebrates dance styles that hail from house and electronic music.

2008 US TV show *So You Think You Can Dance* is syndicated worldwide (eventually to 22 countries), taking hip hop to a bigger audience.

2008 Randy Jackson launches *America's Best Dance Crew* on MTV.

2009 Diversity wins *Britain's Got Talent*.

2009 Jon M. Chu creates *Legion of Extraordinary Dancers* (LXD), where dancers' skills become their superpowers.

2010 American TV series *The LXD* is released.

Did you know?

P. Diddy was once a backing dancer for Big Daddy Kane and Heavy D in the music video 'You Can't See What I Can See' in 1992.

Disco dance

> *'Disco is the best floor show in town.'*
> TRUMAN CAPOTE

What's it all about?

Disco dance, which was inspired by an amalgamation of Latin dance, soul, funk, psychedelic and electronic dances evolved in American cities in the 1970s to disco music (which had only become possible because of new production technology). By the late 1970s many cities had a club-disco scene. The subculture of disco included clubs, dancing, fashion, use of drugs and promiscuity, and the term 'disco inferno' was coined, meaning the combination of these with the nightclub atmosphere of disco and strobe lighting, dry ice and glitterballs. The dance fell into decline in the US partly because the lifestyle was frowned upon, but Euro disco continued developing into the current pop scene that we know today.

Aesthetics: There are a number of moves of varying complexity including the hussle (simplified line dancing), the robot (where the dancer imitates the movement of a robot), bump (where people bump hips to the rhythm), penguin (straight legs to the left and right followed by little jumps), boogaloo (syncopated circular bent-knee movement accompanied by various upper-body angles).

Dress: Disco clothes were often expensive and over the top. At its peak women dressed up in long or mid-length flouncy dresses and men wore tight trousers and shiny shirts. Other clothing included bell bottoms with flares or flounces, platform shoes, gold medallions, shiny buttoned shirts open nearly to the waist, huge curly hair and outrageously bright sunglasses.

Did you know?

In 1973, Karen Lustgarten was the first to codify disco dances and distinguish between freestyle, partner and line dances. Her book The Complete Guide to Disco Dancing *stayed in the* New York Times Best Seller *list for 13 weeks and was translated into Chinese, German and French.*

The songs of a generation

Songs from *Saturday Night Fever* were the soundtrack for the lives of a whole generation. 'Stayin' Alive', 'Jive Talkin', 'Night Fever' and 'Disco Inferno' made the soundtrack album one of the most successful of all time.

Breaking, popping and locking

> *'I dance in the moment not from the past, and yes I know where I come from BUT it doesn't mean I have to be STUCK there.'*
>
> POPIN' PETE

Breaking

What's it all about?

Breaking began on street corners and block parties in Brooklyn and the Bronx, when dancers did their own hip hop thing during the instrumental break of a song. The four characteristic components toprock, downrock, freezes and power moves grew from the adaptation of moves from salsa, merengue and the popular kung fu movies of the time. The dancers themselves became known as breakers, breakboys, breakgirls, b-boys or b-girls.

Aesthetics: A seamless composite of the four characteristic components that is judged by the style or interpretation the individual dancer uses.

Dress: A big part of the culture is the clothing, which is casual with lightweight trainers that have a good grip.

Did you know?

Early breakers wore 1980s shell suits and Adidas shell-toe trainers.

Popping and locking

> 'Becoming a good dancer is not just the learning of complicated moves and routines, it's a philosophy… a way of life.'
>
> GREG 'CAMPBELLOCK JR' POPE

What's it all about?

Popping, first performed by the Electric Boogaloos, is a funk style that uses the rapid contraction and release of muscles so it appears that they are exploding or popping. As a technique this movement is also called a pop or a hit. Locking consists of short, sharp moves with 'locks' or pauses, in a characteristic interpretation which is often syncopated and was first danced by The Lockers. Some say that both styles were also influenced by robots in science fiction television shows like *Lost in Space*.

Aesthetics: Popping styles are tutting, strobing, ticking, dime-stopping, waving and electric boogaloo.

Dress: Varied over the years, for a while lockers had smart styles like zoot suits or T-shirts with baggy trousers, white gloves and soft caps.

Did you know?

Locking is derived from a dance by its creator Don Campbell, called the Campbellock.

Punking, waacking and voguing

> *'Voguing is built from photographic stills.*
> *Punking is built from the screen.'*
>
> SHABBA DOO

What's it all about?

Waacking (also known as punking) originated in the gay community of Los Angeles in the early 1970s, before becoming more widely adopted and then being named waacking (or whacking). Characteristic sharp flicking motions and spinning arms are combined with fast precise footwork and melodramatic stylistic movements inspired by golden-age movie stars such as Lauren Bacall, Marlene Dietrich, Bette Davis or James Dean. Waacking, which puts a strong emphasis on musicality and the interpretation of music and rhythm, was popularised by Shabba Doo, who infused it with locking techniques and promoted it through his stint in local clubs, the Original Soul Train Gang, Broadway, the BBC and his iconic film roles in *Breakin'*, *Breakin' 2: Electric Boogaloo* and the west coast documentary *Entering*. These influenced the creation of a number of other waacking troupes and the dance form gained more mainstream exposure when it featured in *So You Think You Can Dance* in 2011.

Voguing, which grew from punking and evolved further in the Harlem ballroom scene in the 1980s, is a highly stylised form of dancing to music that imitates the characteristic poses struck by a fashion model on a catwalk. It gained ground when featured in Madonna's music video for 'Vogue', the documentary film *Paris is Burning*, and then *America's Best Dance Crew* in 2009.

Aesthetics: Shway-style is a robust codification organically developed by Shabba Doo while waacking practitioners often tend to forget full body motion in favour of the flicking movements.

Dress: Waacking tends to be street smart; voguing dancers wear over-the-top fancy creations to a theme (think science fiction meets Betty Boo).

Did you know?

The House of Suarez holds a Vogue Ball every year in Liverpool. This comprises 'house' groups who dress to a theme. The Twisted Fairy Tale Vogue Ball, managed by a group of men posing as ladies from a knitting club, won Liverpool's Best Annual Event at the Seen Awards in 2011 and 2012 and the opening of their Space Oddity Vogue Ball was performed by Electra, the principal dancer of Starlight Express.

Krumping

What's it all about?

Krumping is an urban dance characterised by its rapid pace, energetic style, and exaggerated and highly aggressive facial movements. Formed as a way to escape the street violence of gang life, it is taught and practiced in close-knit groups called families. It originated in the African American community of South Central Los Angeles in the early 1990s as a fusion of clowning, physical theatre, local and Latin influences, and resembles a rapid-fire full-contact version of breakdance. It has also been popularised through the TV series *Britain's Got Talent* and the film *Street Dance*.

Aesthetics: Jabs, chest pops, arm swings and stomps.

Dress: Loose clothes and baseball hats.

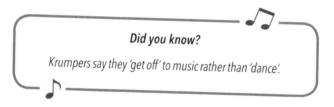

Did you know?

Krumpers say they 'get off' to music rather than 'dance'.

Rude moves

Grinding is a close partner club dance originating in the Caribbean where the hips of both people move in the same circular direction. It may seem like a new rude move but it has been part of both dancehall and Carnival fun for a very long time.

Dancehall

'Move your waist in a slow circle or a figure of eight to Jamaican music fast and slow that sounds good and feels great.'

PARADIGMZ

What's it all about?

Named after the Jamaican dance halls where it evolved, the dance form's development has paralleled that of the music over the past 70 years, although it only developed into a form we would now recognise over the past 40. At first movements tended to come with songs, and the songs were specifically for particular moves. Nowadays, because dancehall is a more mature art, either the dance can come first and the musician can endorse it with a song or the opposite can happen.

At parties, even now, young dancers with Jamaican roots are excited to get a new taste of home and be kept up to date with what is going on; and while they can sing the music, their culture is embodied in the dance. Like other street dances, dancehall is traditionally learnt in this way; first by experience in Jamaican clubs or parties, and only then through words.

Aesthetics: The aesthetics along with the rhythm of the dance lie with the creators. However it is always a literal dance that either stems from an everyday action or is the evolution of a previous dance. These include glue, bogle, whine and dip, tek weh yuself, whine up, badman, sweep.

Dress: Casual and club wear, often with baseball caps.

Did you know?

Dancehall Queen *is a seminal dancehall film about a woman whose street business is threatened by a thug priest and the loan shark she has to borrow money from. She extracts herself from the situation by entering a dancehall competition in disguise, winning the prize money and pitting the two men against each other.*

Urban and street dance game changers

There are so many innovators in the urban dance field that it is difficult to know where to start. From locking to freestyle, dance battles and stage work, there are innovators, excitingly energetic dancers whose cool moves make you gasp, and crews or companies whose mere name evokes a certain style or attitude or groove. Here are just a few:

Dancers

Jojo and Jimmy Dee

Born in the Bronx, Jojo and Jimmy Dee created the pioneering and universally renowned Rock Steady Crew in 1977, an American b-boying crew and hip hop group, which become a hugely influential franchise name for multiple groups in other locations. They used dance battles as a means of auditioning (which they thought of as recruitment) and were given their first big break when photographer Henry Chalfant invited them to the Lincoln Center Outdoors Programme where their dance battle with the Dynamic Rockers was covered by the popular press including *National Geographic*.

Best known for: Jojo is credited with creating the back spin.

Best of the rest

Lil' C (krumper)

Tommy Franzen (choreographer and dancer, *So You Think You Can Dance*)

George Sampson (Britain's Got Talent)

The Jackson 5 (street dance in every video)

Karen Lustgarten (popper)

Paradigmz (contemporary British dancehall legend).

Choreographers and innovators

Toni Basil and Don 'Campbellock' Campbell
Born 1943 and 1951

Toni Basil (born Antonia Christina Basilotta) and Don 'Campbellock' Campbell formed the pioneering street dance group The Lockers in 1971. By 1975 their artistic development had diverged and while they all continued to dance, the levels of commerciality and extent to which they stuck to locking were different.

Best known for: Toni Basil is best known for her number-one hit 'Mickey' (1982) and Don Campbell for creating the dance form locking.

Boogaloo Sam and Popin' Pete
Born 1957 and 1961

After seeing The Lockers on television, Boogaloo Sam was inspired to create his own dance style, and from that arose the street dance crew responsible for the spread of popping and electric boogaloo in Fresno, California, in 1978. His younger brother Popin' Pete joined the following year. They created many of the seminal popping moves. Boogaloo Sam created the old man (a boogaloo-cum-popping stylisation of an old drunk man walking) and the Fresno (a side-to-side movement with body, arm and foot) among other moves. Popin' Pete started his dance education by watching *Soul Train* and doing the robot. He went on to create moves that included crazy legs (based on a dancer with uncoordinated legs).

Best known for: Their popping and electric boogaloo style.

Best of the rest

Breakbot (stimulated hip hop revival)

Shabba Doo (codification of voguing)

Thomas Johnson aka Tommy the Clown (originated the clowning dance form).

Principals, producers and directors

Rennie Harris

Born 1964

Rennie Harris (born Lorenzo Harris) formed the Puremovement company in 1992 and then RHAW (Rennie Harris Awe-Inspiring Works) in 2007. He has received numerous awards for what he calls 'hip hop concert dance' and enjoys breaking expectations. After receiving honorary doctorates from Bates College, Maine and Columbia College, Chicago his company was chosen as cultural ambassadors for President Obama's DanceMotion USA and they toured the Middle East in 2012.

Best known for: Bringing hip hop to the theatre with award-winning shows like *Rome and Jewel*, *Facing Mekka* and *100 Naked Locks*.

Kenrick Sandy and Mikey Asante

Kenrick 'H2O' Sandy and composer Michael 'Mikey J' Asante formed Boy Blue Entertainment, a prominent British hip hop company with a training programme that involves over 150 dancers attending regular classes which feeds their adult and youth company. They have created music for part of the London 2012 Olympics opening ceremony, alongside director Danny Boyle, and won an Olivier Award for their theatre production *Pied Piper* in 2007.

Best known: For their success in creating Boy Blue.

Kate Prince
Born 1974

Kate is the artistic director and producer of ZooNation Dance Company, which she founded in 2002. In May 2010 she became an associate artist at Sadler's Wells and ZooNation became a resident company. Her award-winning production *Into the Hoods* was the longest-running West End dance show in history.

Best known: For bringing the first hip hop dance show to London's West End.

Best of the rest

David LaChapelle (influential photographer)
Jonzi D (promoter and front for Breakin' Convention)
David Mancuso (opened the Loft, a members-only precursor to discos)
Madonna (stimulated various street revivals)
The Village People (Euro disco music and dance)
Diana Ross (combined Motown with disco).

'Competition, of course, is the essence of every aspect of hip hop culture, be it graffiti, emceeing, DJ-ing – what makes it real is the battle.'

KID FREEZE

Did you know?

Michael Jackson's music video for 'Bad' cost a record $2,200,000 to make in 1987. It is 18 minutes long, took six weeks to shoot and was directed by Martin Scorsese. This took over from the 'Thriller' video which, costing $500,000 when it was released in 1983, was considered at the time to be the most expensive video ever made. Both use an innovative choreography of hip hop styles including popping and locking.

Small and silver screen

The Wigan Casino (1977)
Director: Tony Palmer

A documentary about northern soul's most iconic venue and what is arguably still the most famous club in northern England. This documentary, made in 1977 for Granada Television, is a celebration of the joy of breakdancing, expressing the club members' inner satisfaction and fulfilment against a grim background of slums, unemployment and social deprivation; with the dancers in full flow from Friday night non-stop until early Sunday morning, transcending the crushing grind of day to day life.

Fascinating fact: The film featured spins, flips and backdrops in styles that many consider to be a precursor to breakdancing of the 1980s.

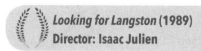

Looking for Langston (1989)
Director: Isaac Julien

This fantasy recreation blends real news footage to celebrate the identity of gay black men in Harlem in the 1920s. There is a mixture of dance, including gay couples waltzing slowly on the dance floor at a smoky 1920s speakeasy and the same tuxedoed men cutting loose to pumping house music, dancing in gleeful mockery as angry policeman and homophobic yobs try to break in.

Fascinating fact: In 1990 Langston Hughes' estate tried to have the film censored for copyright violations in that the film-makers had allegedly not obtained permission to read Hughes' poetry out loud. As a result the sound was turned down when his work was read for many of the films' showings.

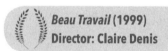

Beau Travail (1999)
Director: Claire Denis

Foreign Legion officer Galoup, played by Denis Lavant, recalls his once glorious life, leading troops in the Gulf of Djibouti and is made jealous by a new recruit. The entire film is dominated by images of synchronised body movements such as military exercises and nightclub dancing.

Fascinating fact: A wonderful example of dance as catharsis, Lavant's isolated legionnaire is last seen (or imagined) alone on a dance floor, suddenly erupting into a convulsive, flailing interpretation of Corona's 'Rhythm of the Night'.

Dave Chappelle's Block Party (2005)
Director: Dave Chappelle

Comedian loads up a bus of residents from his home town in Ohio, everyone goes to Brooklyn and has fun. They go to a concert featuring Kanye West, Big Daddy Kane and the Fugees. The film which combines hip hop, comedy and portraits of real people also has rehearsal footage with some great dance moments too.

Fascinating fact: Although presented as an off-the-wall story, Chappelle has spoken about how it burnt him out, and the film captures the moment in September 2004 when he decides to do things his own way and hang the consequences.

Step Up film series
Director: Anne Fletcher

Mashups of urban, contemporary, salsa, tango and flash mobs in a series of dance stories including romance, competitions, urban dance battles, world championships and fighting the threats of property developers.

Fascinating fact: This was originally to be called *Music High*.

CHAPTER 8

DID YOU KNOW THEY COULD DANCE?

'The dance: a minimum of explanation, a minimum of anecdotes and a maximum of sensations.'

MAURICE BÉJART

Celebrity dancers

It's always great when a friend you didn't think could dance proves you wrong. The thrill is much bigger when it's a star. Here are some big-name celebrities who are also good dancers.

Dancing actors

Christopher Walken
Born 1943

Actor, writer and director Christopher Walken has been in more than 100 films, but originally trained as a dancer in musical theatre and has managed to add a few cool dance moves to each of his roles, most recently as Captain Hook in NBC's live-action production of *Peter Pan*. Allegedly he wanted his dancing immortalised before he got too old and was keen to perform in a music video. Director Spike Jonze put him in Fatboy Slim's 'Weapon of Choice' video which won a number of awards in the 2001 MTV Video Music Awards and the 2002 Grammy Award for the best short-form video.

John Travolta
Born 1954

Actor, dancer and singer John Travolta was nominated for his first Oscar and Golden Globe awards for *Saturday Night Fever* (the film that launched the disco phenomenon in the 1970s). He danced from a very young age, winning a competition for doing the twist before he was 12, and was also taught by Gene Kelly's brother. He danced with Kevin Spacey at the Indian International Film Awards (the Indian Oscars).

The £100,000 suit

In 1977 John Travolta's white suit from Saturday Night Fever *sold for $145,000. The auction house Christie's estimated it at $30,000–$50,000.*

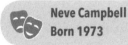

Neve Campbell
Born 1973

Born in Ontario, Canada, Neve Campbell decided to be a dancer when she was six years old after seeing a production of *The Nutcracker*. She graduated from the Erinvale School of Dance to Canada's National Ballet School and appeared in performances of *The Nutcracker* and *Sleeping Beauty*. After a number of nasty dance-related injuries and a stress-related breakdown she started acting instead. She was named the 'television's most believable teenager', became well known for her role in the drama series *Party of Five* and starred as Sidney Prescott in *Scream* in 1996.

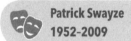

Patrick Swayze
1952-2009

American dancer, actor and singer-songwriter Patrick Swayze, who completed dance training at Harkness Center for Dance in New York and Joffrey Dance Academy in Chicago, was hired as a principal dancer with the Eliot Feld Ballet where he achieved a level of success and was compared with the dancers of the Bolshoi. After ten years and a number of illnesses and injuries he moved to Broadway, where he starred in the musical *Grease*. Supported first by his teacher-choreographer mother and always by his wife, he sizzled through a number of films including a roller-skate ballet film, *Dirty Dancing* and *Ghost*. He died of pancreatic cancer in 2009.

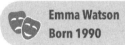

Emma Watson
Born 1990

The English actress who played Hermione in the Harry Potter films listed modern dance and ballet on her official biography a long time before she was given the chance to prove she could dance. Her time to shine as a provocative pole-dancer came in *The Bling Ring*, the preparation for which, she says, included studying Beyoncé's dancing and 'watching a tonne of reality TV'.

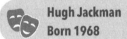

Hugh Jackman
Born 1968

Australian actor and producer who plays Wolverine in the *X-Men* film series is also a Broadway musical singer and dancer. After athletic and impressively nimble dancing on the stage where he presented the 68th Tony Awards he joked that he was 'Wolverine in tap shoes' and his song and dance performance at the 2009 Oscars show was given a standing ovation.

Dancing musicians

> *'Dancing can reveal all the mystery that music conceals.'*
> CHARLES BAUDELAIRE

Music and dance are so intimately related it's not surprising that many musicians have a background in dance, or that they pursue and appreciate innovative dance forms in their music videos. Here are some of the best.

Michael Jackson
1958-2009

Known as the King of Pop, Michael Jackson was the first artist to create dance videos that told a story, included fantastic and innovative dance, and captivated entire audiences irrespective of whether they enjoyed his music. As well as being a consummate dancer and great performer he invented a number of moves. He is particularly famous for his moonwalk (performed to 'Billie Jean' (1982) at the Motown 25: Yesterday, Today, Forever); the dance battle in his 'Beat It' (1982) video, gliding and popping to 'Thriller' (1982) (a genre-breaking music video for its length, dance styles and story) and new dance moves in his 'Smooth Criminal' (1987) music video that included a lean that relied on a specially created shoe.

Madonna
Born 1958

Madonna Ciccone studied dance at the University of Michigan before moving to New York to work as a backing dancer. Since becoming a singer, dance has played a huge part in her videos and live performance. She has given global coverage to many dance forms including voguing ('Vogue', 1990) and krumping ('Hung Up', 2005) by showcasing them in her videos (often flying the experts in from wherever they were in the world to learn from them), while her appearances at major events like the MTV Music Awards and the Super Bowl always feature cutting-edge dance trends.

Beyoncé
Born 1981

Having taken dance classes since elementary school, Beyoncé Giselle Knowles-Carter performed in a number of dance and singing competitions, and began her rise to fame as lead singer of the R&B group Destiny's Child. Her debut solo album *Dangerously in Love* (2003) sold 11 million copies and won five Grammys. Critics love her fast-paced, well-choreographed and presented stage performances, and the way she seeks out new and innovative dance forms, stays true to their essence and responds well to feedback. After searching for five months for the Pantsula dancing Tofo Tofo group (she had seen them on YouTube) she flew them out to teach her their moves and then included them in her dance video 'Run the World (Girls)' in 2011, which went on to win the MTV Video Music Awards Best Choreographed Music Video and the Soul Train Music Awards Best Dance Performance in the same year.

Justin Bieber
Born 1994

Canadian singer, songwriter and dancer Justin Bieber is respected for finding and integrating new dance forms to the world through his videos. 'Somebody to Love' included some of the best street dancers in the world including the Poreotics Crew, the Beat Freaks, the Syrenz, Medea Sirkas and B-Boy Fly. 'Believe' (2012) is a fusion of dance-pop and R&B. He has also performed several sharp routines using different dance styles on *Dancing with the Stars*.

Kate Bush
Born 1958

Singer, songwriter and producer Kate Bush is known for her eclectic music style and unique voice. Her mother was an Irish dancer and it is sometimes said that her style comes as much from the karate lessons she took while at London's Goldsmiths College as from any dance, although it is known that she spent time learning interpretive dance from Lindsey Kemp (who also taught David Bowie). One of her songs from her 1989 album *The Sensual World* is about a woman who dances all night with a man only to discover he is Adolf Hitler.

Shakira
Born 1977

Colombian-born Shakira Isabel Mebarak Ripoll started performing at school where her Latin, Arabic, belly-dancing and rock 'n' roll abilities were already clear. A singer-songwriter, dancer, record producer and model, she was four years old when, first exposed to belly dancing at a local restaurant, she decided to become a dancer. She calls herself a fusion between black and white, pop and rock, her Lebanese father and Spanish-blooded mother, and has expanded her dance repertoire throughout the years. Her well-choreographed performance at the 2014 World Football Championships in Brazil stunned the audience with elements of fast tango and twerking.

Justin Timberlake
Born 1981

After rising to prominence as one of the two lead vocalists and youngest member of the boy band NSYNC, Justin Randall Timberlake has danced his way through music videos and live performances with his own individual panache. In his debut single video he performed Marty Kudelka's laid-back LA new-style choreography which became hugely influential around the world. He appeared in *Star Search* in the 1990s and later won the Dance Recording Award for 'Love Stoned/I Think She Knows' in 2008.

Jennifer Lopez
Born 1969

Latin American dancer and singer Jennifer Lopez (sometimes J-Lo) began her career in musicals and music videos. She started dancing lessons at the age of five, and particularly liked Afro-Caribbean rhythms such as salsa, merengue and bachata, mainstream pop, hip hop and rhythm and blues. She claims that *West Side Story* (1961) was her biggest influence. She was backing dancer for Janet Jackson, a 'Fly Girl' in the TV series *Living Colour*, co-starred with Richard Gere in *Shall We Dance?* (2004) and then produced, created and featured in the reality show *Dance Life*, about dancers trying to make it big. Her music videos and live performances all feature dance routines.

Best of the rest

Tupac (who was very involved in the hip hop scene)
MC Hammer (known for his signature moves the running man and Hammer dance)
Will Smith (whose dances have been copied around the world and who performed a hilarious piece 'the evolution of hip hop' with Jimmy Fallon on *The Tonight Show*).

Did you know?

Irish Dancer Michael Flatley broke his own record for tapping speed in February 1998, by achieving 35 taps per second. He was also recorded in the Guinness Book of Records in 1999 for being the highest paid dancer ($1,600,000 per week at his peak) and for having the highest insurance policy placed on a dancer's legs at $40,000,000.

THE FUTURE
OF DANCE

*'We should consider every day lost on which
we have not danced at least once.'*

FRIEDRICH NIETZSCHE

Dance is a constant. It transcends barriers and enables communication without words. As our different dance forms are shared globally and communities of dance interest become ever more international, based on shared passions for dance forms rather than global boundaries, language or culture, fantastic new unexpected fusions of dance styles will result. That won't take away from the traditional way in which we learn dance, the art will still be passed on from dancer to dancer, but it will broaden the places that our great dance teachers go.

As ever-more passionate people record dance, whether by codification or through video recording, our knowledge of dance will deepen and we will be able to reproduce pure dance forms with confidence, not needing to rely on the sort of archaeology on which those who have recreated historical dances rely. Videography will provide us with constant reference points so we will know which dance forms have stayed true and which have evolved, so the variety of dances we can all draw from will continue to grow as more is shared online, through film and television.

The experience of live dance has already reached a new interactive level. Companies like Punchdrunk blur the lines between performers and audiences by having the performers wear masks and giving the audience free rein. In 2010, 20 French Nao robots performed a series of dance choreographies at the Shanghai Expo, and Klaus Obermaier and various collaborators have been using technology such as lasers, 3D projections and more in their choreographies for many years.

Authentic dance is becoming more important in surprising places too: The Muppets dances are all choreographed and even *Star Wars* aliens dance. *Revenge of the Nerds* (a comedy film about life on an American university campus) shows a future trend; what was for the time a radical combination of dance and technology and even cars have been choreographed to perform ballroom tango with live people at Tower Bridge. The mind boggles as to what might happen next.

While we are always coming up with new ways to inspire an audience through the combination of technology and dance, we are also beginning to have technological help in the creation process. Merce Cunningham, who developed a new form of choreography that he called 'choreography by chance' used a computer programme, developing ideas and choreographies where different aspects of stage, set and choreography were determined by the roll of a dice. The Japanese ballet company Enra has its ballerinas perform with computerised light that responds to their movement. So the interaction of human dancers with technological developments looks set to continue.

Innovative choreographer Crystal Pite already uses every resource possible in her combination of abstract choreography, technology and storytelling, with methods that change between projects. She makes abstract tableaus convey emotional states, such as a group of dancers who blend so well with light projection, screens and lasers that it was impossible to tell which was which. In *Tempest Replica* her choreographies use gestures to demonstrate the intense relationship between Prospero, the monster and his conflicting feelings while *Polaris* (a response to the music of Thomas Adès) involves large numbers of dancers who move together to convey endless miles of burning cold, such as one might find on an ice planet. Her creativity is likely to only continue to grow.

Technology can make the art of choreography more visible too, as some new choreographers embrace it to find deeper ways to reach and engage their audiences. When East London Dance collaborated with choreographer Tony Adigun in 2013 it asked the local community to suggest moves via the social media website Vine, from which Adigun built a performance for his troupe.

Whether the performance is orchestrated by lights, the movements are mirrored by sounds or the scene is created by bodies, dance is becoming far more accessible for the general audience and more popular too. Really there's no telling what the future will bring.

There are some things we can predict though. Every generation of dancers will explore the same basic skills, disciplines and developments in dance as they develop their art. We will always have pure dances like classical ballet and flamenco puro (original flamenco). Yet creative people will continue to push the boundaries of dance in ways we can't anticipate, and dance, like life, will go on. As flamenco dancer Miguel Angel Ruiz once said, 'Life is like dancing… Some will get angry when the rhythm changes. But life changes all the time.'

CONCLUSION

'Dancing is the body talking. You can say anything you want.'
Salah

I hope you have enjoyed this whistle-stop tour of all things dance related. The great news for those of us who love dance is that, after all the ups and downs of history, it has done more than just survive into the twenty-first century, it has flourished and broadened in ways that nobody could have imagined.

Urban dance has gone global; ballroom is as popular as ever; and modern dance keeps fusing with more and more styles. We have access to more great venues than ever and more small dance troupes doing local things too. Teachers are learning better ways to train us and medical discoveries prove that we're doing it right.

So enjoy dancing. It doesn't matter how you get involved, just make sure you do. Dance for fun, to stay fit, to clear your head, for the art, for the social life or because you can't not. Watch dance live if you can, or on TV, online or in the cinema if not.

I hope this book inspires you, intrigues you and makes you want to find out more, and that you enjoy reading it as much as I've enjoyed writing it. Above all I wish you as much pleasure, passion and joy from dance as it has given me.

ABOUT
THE AUTHOR

Carole Edrich is a prize-winning photo journalist who specialises in dance, related culture and travel. Her work, which explores the risks involved in cutting-edge creativity, maintaining ancient traditions and becoming the best, demonstrates her belief that the best way to cover a story is by sharing the experience. So far she has learned 67 different dance forms (before writing this book she thought that was a lot), can interview in Dutch, Spanish and English, teaches dance photography with City Academy, is considered one of the best documentary dance photographers in Europe and published in languages as diverse as Hungarian and Cocani.

For more of Carole's work including posts related to this book visit her blog at www.dancetog.com

ACKNOWLEDGEMENTS

Many thanks to Claire Plimmer and the wonderful people at Summersdale who gave me the opportunity to write this book. Thanks also to; Amir Amirani, Andrea Queens, Carole Dessaigne, Carole Dumenil, Cherry Radclife, Chix Chandaria, Chris White, Debora Bonemei, Debbi Stillwell, Denise Ward, Eleanor Durrant, Eleanor Marriott, Ellie Chapman, Esther Weekes, Funmi Adewole, Gabi Coomber, Gary Leinert, Harry Ward, Hendrick Huthoff, Jade Montoute, Jeremy Hoare, Jim Harwood, Kate Coleman-Brueckenheimer, Kamara Grey, Kele Baker, Kerrin Leoni, Kerry Fletcher, Kim Sheard, Lemington Ridley, Marv TheRadio, Melodie Gina Brannan, Mariano Gutierrez Alarcon, Milo Miles, Natasha Khamjani, Nejc Jus, Norman Spence, Nuria Garcia, Popin' Pete, Rosi Reed, Rowena Ritchie, Sasha C Damjanovski, Sarah Spencer, Sean Graham, Sean Murricane, Sep Dashti, Shabba Doo, Sherrill Maron, Sideshow Male, Simon Hyde, Simon Selmon, Thomas Michael Voss, Thomas Talwa Presto, Tim Baggaley, Ushma Patel, Vanessa Downie and Vera King who provided their expertise or helped me decide which of the thousands of interesting facts, great quotes and films should go into the book and which should not.

THE JOY OF CINEMA

GRAHAM TARRANT

THE JOY OF CINEMA
Graham Tarrant

ISBN: 978 1 84953 720 9   Hardback   £9.99

No art passes our conscience in the way film does, and goes directly to our feelings.

INGMAR BERGMAN

This miscellany, packed with fascinating film history, a treasury of trivia and in-depth exploration of the genres, blockbusters and stars of the movie world, is perfect for any film buff who loves the storytelling magic of the silver screen.

Have you enjoyed this book?
If so, why not write a review on your favourite website?

If you're interested in finding out more about our books, find
us on Facebook at **Summersdale Publishers** and follow us
on Twitter at **@Summersdale**.